D1177141

God Is Calling His People To Forgiveness

BY
GENE LILLY

Published by
Hunter Ministries Publishing Co.
1600 Townhurst
Houston, Texas 77043

Canadian Office
Hunter Ministries Publishing Company of Canada
P.O. Box 30222, Station B
Calgary, Alberta, Canada T2M 4P1

First Printing July 1977.............10,000
Second Printing Aug. 1977 25,000

Scripture quotations are taken from:
The Authorized King James Version (KJV)

ISBN 0-917726-15-4

TABLE OF CONTENTS

Page

Gene and Phyllis are in full-time evangelism and travel all over the nation and into foreign countries and islands. God is mightily using them.

My thanks to George Clouse for his generous aid in the compiling of this book.

INTRODUCTION

by Stephen Strang, Editor of
CHARISMA Magazine

One of the most important truths a Christian can learn is the freedom and release that results from forgiving. Yet this truth escapes attention in most churches even though Christ taught it many times.

One of his most familiar lessons is in Matthew 18 about a servant whose master forgave a debt of what would be $20 million in our money. The servant turned around and refused to forgive a fellow servant a measly $17 debt, and had him thrown into prison.

For years I was outraged that a servant who was forgiven so much would be so unforgiving. I never realized I was worse.

The light dawned when I heard Gene Lilly minister the message you are about to read.

He asked if any of us had ever been wronged in some small way and harbored unforgiveness.

I knew I had. I resented college friends who borrowed and kept my used textbooks; I was hurt over fellow believers who wouldn't give back a favorite cassette. I even was still piqued because my younger brother, years ago, had stolen most of my penny collection — one by one so I wouldn't notice — so he could buy candy.

When Gene retold the story about the unforgiving servant, the truth about forgiveness came flooding into a darkroom of my understanding. It exposed all my unforgiveness. Suddenly I contrasted my not forgiving my little brother for those pennies he took to the anger, covetousness, envy, gluttony, lust, pride and sloth I had been forgiven by Christ on Calvary, and I knew I was more unforgiving than that servant.

I'm not normally emotional, but the tears of regret that welled up inside when I realized my unforgiveness, spilled over my face that night.

Gene led us in a prayer for forgiveness and I asked Jesus to forgive any malice, slander or anything I had in my heart against anyone.

Then I asked Jesus to show me those I had refused to forgive. I couldn't believe how fast the Holy Spirit brought to my mind experience after experience of the times when I had refused to forgive someone. However, there was one experience which was more painful than the others because the *need* for forgiveness was greater.

A Christian brother to whom I had been very closely related, a fine young man whom I helped establish in his ministry, had turned his back on me [to my way of thinking], and had broken our close relationship. To avoid the unpleasant situation that developed from becoming more unpleasant, I withdrew. I felt I had been the peacemaker. Yet I was very hurt by the experience, and the very thought of the events that took place made my stomach churn.

What the Holy Spirit showed me that night hurt even more. He showed me *I* was at fault. It was *I*, not my brother, who had created the circumstances which eventually led to our broken friendship.

My strong-willed personality made us clash. After a few clashes, it was *I* who allowed the situation to get worse by not turning it over to the Lord. *I* worked out a solution — *I* withdrew. But that wasn't the Lord's solution and I *knew* I had to ask my brother to forgive me.

The next day I cleared an hour in my schedule and went to his office to do what I knew would be difficult — to ask his forgiveness.

The Lord had been showing me, I told him, that I had wronged him and I wanted him to forgive me.

I expected him to say he'd been wrong too and that he wanted me to forgive him, but he didn't. Instead, he said he had already forgiven me — months before.

Then I understood that I really *had* been wrong. My brother realized it long before I did. When I asked him to forgive me, he did. We prayed together, and as I left, only 10 minutes after I came, we embraced as brothers once again.

When I returned to my office I sat alone for several minutes and wept. I thanked God for the release I felt in my spirit. It was as if a rope had been around my heart, making me feel tight inside. But now it was released; I felt peace. The release I felt was almost as great as the release I felt when Christ saved me from my sin.

I had forgiven, and as I did, Christ forgave me for the wrong I had done.

Chapter One

SEEING JESUS IN YOURSELF

When you can see Jesus in yourself, you can start seeing Jesus in others. *In Christ,* you are redeemed, set free, sanctified, prosperous, and righteous. The Bible teaches that *you have all spiritual blessings dwelling in you right now!*

Let me show you something on spiritual blessings from John 14:23;

> *Jesus answered and said unto him, If a man love me, he will keep my words: and my Father will love him, and we will come unto him, and make our abode with him.*

Most people are waiting to die to go to the Father's house. They are missing all the benefits of living in his house right now!

Jesus and the Father are alive in us, therefore, we are in our Father's house now. *"For in him dwelleth all the fullness of the Godhead bodily" (Col. 2:9).*

Oftentimes we do not consider ourselves to be saints. Instead we consider ourselves to be sinners. This is *not* what the word of God teaches. Let's look at it logically. When a man works at being a plumber, he is called a plumber. When he works as a carpenter, he is called a carpenter. It does not necessarily mean that he is a perfect plumber or a perfect carpenter. He may not have all the answers in his particular trade.

The same truth applies to you and me. If you are a Christian, you are working at being a saint, therefore you are called a saint. (You are no longer practicing to be a sinner, so you should not be called a sinner.) All Christians were called saints by Paul in his writings to the churches at Ephesus, Corinth, etc.

The New Testament states approximately 140 times that we are *in Christ!* Start seeing yourself as you are *in Jesus.* Confess what you are *in Christ* and it will change your life. Jesus paid a tremendous price for us to have all spiritual blessings.

Whether you realize it or not you are a valuable possession. Compared to what you were before you were saved, you are a mansion. Inside that mansion dwells God's possession.

God's only interest is in *his people.* Reading through the scriptures you will find that God is interested in his people because the glory of the Lord is made manifest in them.

I Peter 2:9 says it best:

> *But ye are a chosen generation, a royal priesthood, an holy nation, a peculiar people . . .*

A different people! We need to grasp that!

If we get a little persecution or something goes wrong, we start rebuking the devil. The saints in the book of Acts just said, "LORD, SEND MORE ANOINTING!"

In the fourth chapter of Acts the priests, the captain of the temple, and the Sadducees had released Peter and John. They had been told if they said one more word about Jesus, they were going to be beaten until there was nothing left of them! Listen to the reply:

> *And when they heard that, they lifted up their voice to God with one accord, and*

> *said, Lord, thou art God, which hast made*
> *heaven, and earth, and the sea, and all*
> *that in them is:*
>
> *Who by the mouth of thy servant David*
> *hast said, Why did the heathen rage, and*
> *the people imagine vain things?*
>
> *The kings of the earth stood up, and*
> *the rulers were gathered together against*
> *the Lord, and against his Christ.*
>
> *For of a truth against thy holy child*
> *Jesus, whom thou hast anointed, both*
> *Herod, and Pontius Pilate, with the*
> *Gentiles, and the people of Israel, were*
> *gathered together,*
>
> *For to do whatsoever thy hand and thy*
> *counsel determined before to be done.*
>
> *And now, Lord, behold their threaten-*
> *ings: and grant unto thy servants, that*
> *with all boldness they may speak thy*
> *word,*
>
> *By stretching forth thine hand to heal;*
> *and that signs and wonders may be done*
> *by the name of thy holy child Jesus. (Acts*
> *4:24-30)*

They just prayed for *more anointing:* they didn't pray
for the devil to be bound. They simply said, "Lord,
anoint us more that we can proclaim it a little louder,"
with more confidence and more boldness than ever before, and look what happened!

Verse 31:

> *And when they had prayed, the place was*
> *shaken where they were assembled to-*
> *gether; and they were all filled with the*
> *Holy Ghost, and they spake the word of*
> *God with boldness. (Acts 4:31)*

We should be praying for *more anointing!* We are coming into a time of persecution and there are going to be a

lot of people who will never win one single soul, because they will spend all their time binding the devil.

Persecution has to come to get the "lukewarm" either hot or cold. It's much more fun being hot than lukewarm. I know from experience that it used to be miserable being cold and I suppose it still is.

It is time we give the Lord complete control of our life and ask him *to live through us.* Either Christ is alive in us or he isn't! It is either his life that is living in us or we are nothing.

Jesus often gets the blame for things he isn't doing. We need to realize just where the problem is.

Someone came to me recently and told me they were having a problem with God. I have never had a problem with God. I have had problems with myself and I have had problems with the devil, but GOD HAS ALWAYS BEEN ABSOLUTELY RIGHT!

There definitely is such a thing as a "glorious church without spot or wrinkle." Some preachers teach that this means just a spiritual church. I'VE GOT NEWS FOR THEM! God *will* raise up a glorious church on this earth without spot or wrinkle!

It *will* be victorious and it *will* be glorious. The *power* of the Lord is going to reside in it!

We need the power of the Holy Ghost like they had it, when the building was shaken and they spoke the word of God with boldness. Then we would not need all our petty rules that men have set up.

When you spray insect repellant on mosquitoes, they leave. In the same way, you can let the love of the Lord flow on some people and it is just like putting repellant on them. They leave! The love of the Lord can be a repellant if you are not willing to receive it.

For the church to ever come into the place of power that God wants, we must reckon with forgiveness.

I have taught extensively on the subject of forgiveness. It is a fact that forgiveness is a *necessity* for living a victorious Christian life. Resentment and unforgiveness are the cancer of the mind, the emotions, and the body. It literally eats away at you.

There are many Christians today who are not free. The reason they are not is because they do not understand or practice forgiveness. *"And ye shall know the truth, and the truth shall make you free" (John 8:32),* is a verse we often hear quoted.

You can hear that from the pit of Hell! I have heard *that* from some of the very worst cults. I have heard the voodoo worshippers in the islands in the Obie Temple repeating, *"Ye shall know the truth, and the truth shall make you free."* BUT, THAT IS NOT ALL JESUS SAID!

He says:

> *Then said Jesus to those Jews which be-*
> *lieved on him, If ye continue in my word,*
> *then are ye my disciples indeed; And ye*
> *shall know the truth, and the truth shall*
> *make you free (John 8:31-32).*

Do you abide in the word? Many times the devil will get your head filled with lies and that will be what you are abiding in. In this case, you are not free. You are bound! Many people think they are in freedom when they are not. The devil has their mind full of junk and they are living by that junk. They have never renewed their mind with the word of God. They have never allowed themselves to be set free!

Chapter Two

DO NOT JUDGE

One of the areas in which we may not have been set
free is *unforgiveness.* In John 12:47, Jesus said a very
interesting thing:

> *And if any man hear my words, and be-*
> *lieve not, I judge him not: for I came not*
> *to judge the world, but to save the world.*

We were mindful of this verse when we ministered in
the Cayman Islands. We went into places where no
preacher had been in twenty years. We prayed for the
sick and gave them food. We did not worry about what
would come next. We didn't judge them. We simply told
them that the Lord had provided it and before long they
wanted to know about Jesus. As we shared about Jesus,
people started getting saved.

If anyone hears my sayings and does not keep them, I
do not judge him. I want you to think on that statement.
As you think on it, it will become more important to
you.

Jesus is alive in his body. If you are a born-again,
spirit-filled believer, the *power* and *authority* of Jesus
Christ is alive in you. When that power is in you, all
spiritual blessings are in you.

Where? IN YOU!

All spiritual blessings are just the thickness of the flesh away from you.

If you have never been born again, if you have never received Jesus, there is nothing inside you except a big empty hole. Even so, Jesus said, I do not judge any man. There is a day of judgment coming, but it is not here yet.

Jesus had the same power to judge then that he will have at the day of judgment.

He had the power to judge *anyone* at that time. We are operating in the *power* of the name of Jesus. It is just like a power of attorney. A power of attorney legally gives us the right to sign another's name.

Jesus said, *"All power is given unto me in heaven and in earth" (Matt 28:18).* Then he said, "Go . . ." What we often try to do is to set up the day of judgment now. If we start judging people (operating in the power of the name of Jesus), then what happens? We are out of his will and peace disappears. Judging is *not* the job Jesus called us to do.

In the same way we can speak healing and deliverance into people; we can also speak condemnation, judgment, and bondage into them. Remember, we are operating under the same authority.

Jesus' teaching on forgiveness was so strong that in John 20:23, he said: *"Whosoever sins ye remit, they are remitted unto them; and whosoever sins ye retain, they are retained."*

That's heavy, isn't it? Those sins you remit are remitted and those you retain are retained. Who was he talking to? The church! *Us!* In other words, we can retain or bind sins for someone else.

We hold people in bondage. We hold ourselves in bondage. Jesus taught more on forgiveness in Matthew 18:23-27:

> *Therefore is the kingdom of heaven likened unto a certain king, which would take account of his servants.*

> *And when he had begun to reckon, one was brought unto him, which owed him ten thousand talents.*

Ten thousand talents was valued at between ten and twenty million dollars. I would say that was a pretty substantial debt.

> *But forasmuch as he had not to pay, his lord commanded him to be sold, and his wife, and children, and all that he had, and payment to be made.*
>
> *The servant therefore fell down, and worshipped him, saying, Lord, have patience with me, and I will pay thee all.*
>
> *Then the lord of that servant was moved with compassion, and loosed him, and forgave him the debt.*

Now at this point he was a free man. Hallelujah! Free! But continuing on in verse 28:

> *But the same servant went out, and found one of his fellowservants, which owed him an hundred pence; and he laid hands on him, and took him by the throat, saying, Pay me that thou owest.*

An hundred pence in today's money is less than $20.00, probably about $17.00. He had just been forgiven a debt of probably more than ten million dollars. The fellowservant owed him seventeen dollars and he was going to choke him to death for it. Can you picture that? Verses 29-30 say:

> *And his fellowservant fell down at his feet, and besought him, saying, Have patience with me, and I will pay thee all.*
>
> *And he would not: but went and cast him into prison, till he should pay the debt.*

So the free man put the other one in jail . . . *in bondage!*

So when his fellowservants saw what was done, they were very sorry, and came and told unto their lord all that was done.

Then his lord, after that he had called him, said unto him, O thou wicked servant, I forgave thee all that debt, because thou desiredst me:

Shouldest not thou also have had compassion on thy fellowservant, even as I had pity on thee?

And his lord was wroth, and delivered him to the tormentors, till he should pay all that was due unto him.

So likewise shall my heavenly Father do also unto you, if ye from your hearts forgive not every one his brother their trespasses (vss. 31-35).

There are lots of people in the deliverance ministry today. Even so, there are people in bondage because they have not forgiven. You are not going to *keep* your deliverance unless *you forgive.*

Unforgiveness is a luxury of the flesh. A luxury you cannot afford to have. It makes your flesh feel good at the time, but it will literally destroy you.

The first servant came out totally forgiven. *Free!* But he grabbed his fellowservant, began choking him and threw him in jail. Then *he* was thrown in jail. They both ended up in prison. They both ended up bound.

The servant that was forgiven could have taken his fellowservant by the hand and said, I forgive you. They could have walked through life together totally *free!* Instead they both ended up in bondage.

Do you see how we can keep someone else bound?

As long as we have not forgiven someone, we are keeping the church from coming together. We have kept that person in bondage as well as ourselves. There is a lot more to forgiving than just involving ourselves. In forgiving we are releasing the other person as well as ourselves.

Jesus said, if you retain that sin, it is retained. Jesus hung on a cross and said, *"Father, forgive them . . ."* *(Luke 23:34).* He forgave them!

When Jesus called Lazarus from the grave, he called him by name. If he had not, all the dead would have come forth. When Jesus asked the Father to forgive them their sin, all sin was forgiven. The church is now operating in the name of Jesus. Now who needs to be doing the forgiving?

Jesus forgave then, and now it is up to us. We are the only ones who can retain sin against someone else. It is time we started reckoning with what God says about forgiveness and relationships.

I know that sometimes it is hard to do what the Lord asks. If you want victory in your life, the truth will set you free. The truth will set you *totally* free. When we start realizing that, we will be willing to do what God asks.

The next thing I would like for you to understand is that it makes no difference what happened to cause unforgiveness. It makes no difference who was right or wrong. It is totally immaterial. The only one it is important to be right with is God. When you are right with him, you will be right with your brother and sister.

Your relationship horizontally is the same as your relationship vertically. Your relationship with your brother and sister is in direct proportion to your relationship with your heavenly Father. John said in I John 4:20, *"If a man say, I love God, and hateth his brother, he is a liar . . ."*

Many people have already made up their minds. They have completely justified their feelings of unforgiveness or resentment. They say things like, "I had a right to . . ." or "It was his fault . . ." or maybe, "She caused it all . . ."

Was Jesus wronged? He was the only one who never did any wrong to anyone! He was completely right! Yet he said, *"Father, forgive them."*

Have you ever read the sermon that Stephen preached in the book of Acts? He was *really* anointed. He preached of Abraham and his descendants, on down through Moses. He spoke of the tabernacle in the wilderness. Then he told of Solomon building a temple for God.

Finally he said that God does not dwell in temples made with hands, but in us. He accused the listeners of being stiff-necked in heart and ears, and said they always resisted the Holy Spirit, even as their fathers did.

When they heard these things they became angry and started berating Stephen. Acts 7:55 says: *"But he, being full of the Holy Ghost, looked up steadfastly into heaven, and saw the glory of God, and Jesus standing on the right hand of God."*

He told them what he saw and they became even more angry. They grabbed him and dragged him from the city. They laid their coats at Saul's feet (he later became the great apostle Paul who wrote a major portion of the New Testament) and began to stone him.

Do you know what Stephen did then? He knelt down and cried with a loud voice, *"Lord, lay not this sin to their charge."*

Did they do Stephen wrong? Certainly they did! He was the only one in that crowd who was right, yet they stoned him to death. He looked up and when he saw Jesus he said, don't blame them . . . *forgive them!*

It does not make any difference who is right and who is wrong. The "natural mind" says someone else is wrong! Get that completely out of your head. This is the devil's way of justifying it in your own mind.

If Jesus had not said, "Father forgive them," as he hung on the cross, we would still be in the same shape as the people were before he died. But the fact remains, *he* did speak those words. He shed his blood, and his word is still here! He was right, and still he *forgave* us!

Peter wrote on this subject in I Peter 2:19-21:

> *For this is thankworthy, if a man for conscience toward God endure grief, suffering wrongfully.*
>
> *For what glory is it, if, when ye be buffeted for your faults, ye shall take it patiently? but if, when ye do well, and suffer for it, ye take it patiently, this is acceptable with God.*
>
> *For even hereunto were ye called: because Christ also suffered for us, leaving us an example, that ye should follow his steps:*

If you do well, and suffer anyway, that is most acceptable with God! That tells us to forgive, regardless of who is at fault, and if we forgive when it is *not* our fault then we will receive glory!

Jesus was our example in forgiveness. We are to follow *his* example and forgive, regardless of who is at fault.

Let's look at some more of Jesus' teaching. The account of his teaching known as the Sermon on the Mount begins in Matthew 5:23:

> *Therefore if thou bring thy gift to the altar, and there rememberest that thy brother hath aught against thee;*

... Remember he is saying that your brother has something against you! He is not talking about you having something against your brother, but that you know he has something against you. Have you ever been caught in that situation?

You knew there was a *broken relationship* between you and someone, but you really did not have anything in your heart against them. They might have been totally wrong. Still you remember your brother has something against you. Verse 24 says:

> *Leave there thy gift before the altar, and go thy way; first be reconciled to thy brother, and then come and offer thy gift.*

Do you see what God is saying?

When we know that somebody has something against us, God says, don't come around with your hallelujahs and praises until you get that relationship *right*.

Christianity is not a religion of right doctrine, but a religion of right relationship!

The Bible says to go your way first and be reconciled, then come in. Come in and praise God when you are free.

Release your brother!

By going to him and straightening out relationships you not only release him, but also secure your own release!

A couple of years ago I was with three Christian brothers in Texas. One of them felt a burden to start a new work for the Lord in Texas. We got together and prayed about it.

After seeking the guidance of the Holy Spirit we did not feel that all four of us were to be involved. The three of us felt that the one who wanted to start the work should do so and the three of us should pray and do anything that was necessary to help. After this decision we each went our own way.

There didn't seem to be anything harmful and the three of us never gave it much thought. However, the brother who remained in Texas had Satan (the accuser of the brethren) whispering in his ear:

"Those guys don't want anything to do with you, that's why they won't have anything to do with this work."

That thought fed on his mind and his spirit.

I did not know what the problem was with him but I did know that something was wrong. (Remembering that thy brother hath aught against thee.) The Lord kept bringing that scripture to my mind.

Finally, I got in contact with the other two brothers and asked them to meet me in Texas. Upon meeting, we called our minister friend and asked him to have lunch with us while we were in town. He agreed.

We met at a restaurant. We all ate, laughed, shared and had a marvelous time.

Then I said, "We are not in fellowship anymore. I don't know why, but that doesn't matter. Whatever I have done to you that is wrong I want you to forgive me. Whatever has hurt your feelings, I ask your forgiveness."

With that he shared his story and unburdened his heart. It wasn't a matter of whether I was innocent of wrong doing or not. What did matter was that he forgave me! You see, we do not have to prove we are right; we have to prove we are willing to forgive.

Our relationship is completely renewed and it flourishes today, thanks to complete forgiveness through Christ Jesus.

Chapter Three

LOVE YOUR ENEMIES

Jesus is coming back for a glorified body; a church without spot or wrinkle. A church where the barriers between brothers have been broken down and we are not fighting one another. We do not have to agree on everything because doctrinally we are going to have some differences. But, we can agree that Jesus is Lord and that he is the only way to heaven.

If we can keep our mind and eyes on Jesus and Jesus in our brothers and sisters, we can get along with each other a whole lot better. I believe that often we are not hearing much of what God has to say to us because we are not willing to receive ministry from others. You can never receive anything from anybody you are not willing to receive from or submit to. You must be willing to become a servant to, or become less than, that person.

Jesus became the least to become the greatest. He called us to serve. When we wait upon the Lord, we are serving him so that our strength will be renewed. Then we will receive the power to do the work he has asked us to do.

Isaiah 40:31 teaches this principle:

But they that wait upon the Lord shall renew their strength; they shall mount up

>*with wings as eagles; they shall run, and*
>*not be weary; and they shall walk, and*
>*not faint.*

Jesus taught about forgiveness in Matthew 6 when he gave us the Lord's prayer. He taught us to forgive our debtors as *we* are forgiven our debts.

He went on to say that if we forgive men their transgressions, our Heavenly Father will also forgive us. But if we do not forgive men, then our Heavenly Father will not forgive us.

I see some Christians who are beaten down by the devil. They are carrying a load of sin because their heart is filled with resentment, hate, and unforgiveness. I do not believe that Jesus could have made it much clearer. His teaching about forgiveness dwells around the things we say. A prime example is in Matthew 12:34-37:

>*O generation of vipers, how can ye, being*
>*evil, speak good things? for out of the*
>*abundance of the heart the mouth*
>*speaketh.*
>
>*A good man out of the good treasure of*
>*the heart bringeth forth good things: and*
>*an evil man out of the evil treasure*
>*bringeth forth evil things.*
>
>*But I say unto you, That every idle*
>*word that men shall speak, they shall give*
>*account thereof in the day of judgment.*
>
>*For by thy words thou shalt be justi-*
>*fied, and by thy words thou shalt be con-*
>*demned.*

In the ministry of healing and deliverance you can hear people getting well! I mean that. You can literally *hear* them getting well!

There was a young Viet Nam veteran who came to me about a year ago. He had lost his sight. His body was disfigured physically as well as spiritually; he was almost completely destroyed. He was filled with hate.

Praise Jesus, he got serious about God and Jesus saved him! He was baptized and filled with the Holy Spirit a short time afterwards.

A land mine had gone off near him which had destroyed his ear drum. It caused his ears to ring constantly. Since he gave his life to Jesus, God healed his ear drums and stopped the ringing.

He also had one arm that had been operated on and it was about two inches shorter than the other. It has been growing out to become even with the other.

By just listening to that young man talk, you can *hear* him getting well. His *spirit* has been healed and his *mind* is being renewed. Healing and deliverance is coming forth FROM HIS MOUTH. Rivers of living water are pouring forth from his body and more of his healing is being manifested. That man will be completely whole because he is letting God do a work in him. What he is speaking is truth!

You see, faith comes from hearing and hearing from the word of God. Most of us read that verse and think we need to get to church to hear our pastor preach the word. (And don't be mistaken, we do need to get to church and hear our pastor.) But did you know that you learn three times faster when you hear it from your own mouth?

We need to be *speaking* the word that our faith might be built. That does not mean that you don't go to church. It only means that all the time you are not in church you should be confessing the word of God.

Jesus taught many practical and necessary principals in the Sermon on the Mount. In Luke 6:27-28, he said:

> *But I say unto you which hear, Love your enemies, do good to them which hate you,*
>
> *Bless them that curse you, and pray for them which despitefully use you.*

It is time we realized that a lot of the people in our past are the very ones Jesus is describing.

Quit binding the devil until you learn to love!

There is no need to bind the devil until you learn to bless those that curse you and pray for those that despitefully use you. Until you get in the will of God, you may as well forget about binding the devil!

Sometimes we are trying to take authority over something when we do not have any authority. We are not in the flow of God. When somebody is cursing us, we want to curse him back so we bind the devil. Do you think the Lord is going to bless us in a case like that?

The Lord says for us to *bless* those that *curse* us!

When we do that, then we can bind the devil and take authority over him. But until we bless those who despitefully use us, we cannot bind the devil.

Jesus continued teaching in Luke 6:29-35:

> *And unto him that smiteth thee on the one cheek offer also the other; and him that taketh away thy cloak forbid not to take thy coat also.*
>
> *Give to every man that asketh of thee; and of him that taketh away thy goods ask them not again.*
>
> *And as ye would that men should do to you, do ye also to them likewise.*
>
> *For if ye love them which love you, what thank have ye? for sinners also love those that love them.*
>
> *And if ye do good to them which do good to you, what thank have ye? for sinners also do even the same.*
>
> *And if ye lend to them of whom ye hope to receive, what thank have ye? for sinners also lend to sinners, to receive as much again.*
>
> *But love ye your enemies, and do good, and lend, hoping for nothing again; . . .*

Do you remember the last time you got mad at some Christian who did not return your cassette tapes?

Lend, expecting nothing in return, Jesus said.

I remember a couple of years ago when I was ministering in my home church, Calvary Assembly, I brought out this very thought. My wife, Phyllis, was in the congregation and the Holy Spirit made that statement real to her.

Lend, expecting nothing in return.

Phyllis thought of the many times she had complained about people failing to return her many tapes and books she had bought and loaned.

"Oh, God," she prayed. "Forgive me for complaining. And I *forgive* each person who has failed to return anything whatsoever they have borrowed from me."

This was a simple but sincere prayer, whispered as I was preaching. The service was over and Phyllis forgot to mention to me the prayer of forgiveness she had whispered.

The next Sunday morning as we went in the front door of the church a friend called,

"Phyllis, I have something for you," and she came running up to us. "I was looking through the chest of drawers yesterday and found these three cassette tapes of yours," and she handed them over to Phyllis.

"I'm terribly sorry about having them so long, but I had completely forgotten about them. Will you forgive me?"

Phyllis had a knowing smile on her lips. "Yes," she said, "I certainly will forgive you."

She handed me the tapes and we started on into the church. A friend stopped me and said, "I'm returning the book Phyllis loaned me last month. It was sure good. Sorry I was so slow about returning it." With that he handed me a book. Again Phyllis smiled.

From that point forward I lost count. Person after person came up, one with two books, one with half a dozen tapes and four books, others with one or more tapes or books. It was unbelievable!

"What's going on?" I asked Phyllis. Again she smiled that knowing smile.

By the time we got settled in our seats and the service began it looked like we were ready to start a library right there in the pew. We must have had a pile of two dozen tapes and a dozen or more books. It looked as if everybody in the church had at least one tape or book to give back to us.

As soon as the service was over I took off for the car, with my arms full of tapes and books!

"What is going on?" I insisted. "I've never seen anything like this and all you do is grin and look like the cat that swallowed the canary."

"You remember when you were preaching on forgiveness the other day?" I nodded. "You mentioned that Jesus said to lend, expecting nothing in return!" Again I nodded.

"Well, I prayed and forgave each and every person who had failed to return things they had borrowed," she said. "When I forgave them, it must have released them. I must have had them bound by my complaining against them!"

What a truth she had learned about forgiveness! Now I could understand what had been going on. Now I understood why all the tapes and books had suddenly started flowing back. Unforgiveness had stopped up the channel but forgiveness had unclogged the pipes.

I went to another person's house recently who almost fell out of fellowship with God because someone had not returned a special new translation of the Bible they had borrowed.

If we would give and not worry about, or even expect, anything in return, we would not get into this type of difficulty. That is what Jesus is teaching in the sixth chapter of Luke. After he said: *"Lend, hoping for nothing again: . . ."* He continued in Luke 6:35 and 36:

> *And your reward shall be great, and ye shall be the children of the Highest: for he*

> *is kind unto the unthankful and to the
> evil.*
>
> *Be ye therefore merciful, as your
> Father also is merciful.*

That was Jesus saying, "He *is kind unto the unthankful
and to the evil."*

The problem with us is that we want to be kind to
everybody who is the absolute image and likeness of the
Lord Jesus Christ. But what about the ones who are not
quite there yet?

Even more important than that, what about those
drunks down the street who are not even saved? What
about the ones doing the opposite of what God wants?
What about the ones involved in witchcraft? What about
one of the mediums in the local spiritualist church?

A lot of Christians are binding them with their condemnation and making it far more difficult for them to
get free. Be merciful, just as your Father is merciful. Jesus
continued in verse 37:

> *Judge not, and ye shall not be judged:
> condemn not, and ye shall not be con-
> demned: forgive, and ye shall be for-
> given . . .*

Why do you suppose Jesus said that? Because he knew
what was going to happen to us when we started doing it.
He knew that when we judge and condemn people, we
place a binding on them, restricting their freedom to
come to Jesus.

Right at the end of that quote Jesus said,

> *. . . and ye shall be forgiven . . .*
>
> *Give, and it shall be given unto you;
> good measure, pressed down, and shaken
> together, and running over, shall men give
> into your bosom. For with the same meas-
> ure that ye mete withal it shall be meas-
> ured to you again. (Verse 38).*

I know some Christians today who wonder why they
cannot fellowship with anybody. It's because they have

judged about half the people in town and it has come
right back on them. It came back on them because they
started binding other people and ended up getting into
bondage themselves.

Jesus' teaching was so strong that I don't think most
people have ever begun to grasp what he said about
relationships with one another. In the area of forgiveness
it is quite clear that Jesus was not talking about our being
right. He did not deal with our being right, he was talking
about *us* forgiving when we are right and the other person
is wrong.

One man who found the truth in this principle is one
of our best friends, George Clouse. George is a former
Methodist who received the baptism of the Holy Spirit
four years ago and is one of the most gentle Christians I
know. George's vivacious wife, Mary Jo, is our able administrative assistant.

George and Mary Jo have a beautiful Christian home
and two well-behaved teenagers.

One of George's greatest heartaches is that he reared
his three grown children in an un-Christian home because
he did not know Jesus until after they left home.

Still, George *believed* his children would become
Christians. Shortly after this, his two daughters and their
husbands came to know the Lord. But his oldest son, Bill,
seemed a hopeless case.

Bill is a big burly man who loved big motorcycles and
who had worked, among other jobs, as a bouncer in a bar.
Religion was the farthest thing from his mind, and he
wouldn't even come near a church. This was, of course, a
big disappointment to George and Mary Jo.

The night I preached about forgiveness, it dawned on
George that he had been condemning Bill and his wife for
not living right.

As soon as the service was over George and Mary Jo
joined together, *forgiving* Bill and his wife.

"We were judging and condemning when we should have been forgiving," George told me later. "We changed things that night and have never condemned again."

It was less than a week after "forgiving" them that Bill's wife came to church with George and Mary Jo for the first time. The following week Bill went by his dad's office and talked with him for over an hour about the reality of God and what was missing in his life. George challenged him to attend church for four straight Sunday mornings and test and see if God would meet his needs. He accepted the challenge.

Four Sundays went by and each Sunday morning Bill was there as he had promised. The following Wednesday night, just after ten o'clock, Bill telephoned his dad, and George led him to the Lord over the phone. The next Sunday night Bill and his wife were baptized in water and came up from the water eager to serve the Lord. The condemnation and judgment by the parents had been felt by and resisted by the children.

Salvation was theirs all because they were set free!

George loosed them from the bonds of condemnation. He loosed them from the power of unforgiveness so they could come to the Lord!

Praise God! It works!

Mary Jo's mother called her and said she had not slept well the night before because a group of young men had gathered outside her house under the street light and "carried on" most of the night. She said they had been doing this for quite some time, and she had even called the police a couple of times. They would leave before the police arrived so she had not been able to get anything done about it.

Mary Jo, having found the truth in forgiveness, told her mother that she needed to forgive them and loose them. Mom certainly wasn't too enthusiastic about that but she agreed to do it anyway.

Do you know, that solved the problem!

After she prayed and forgave them, they immediately changed their ways and one of them was saved the next week. Now Mom is a believer, too, in the power of forgiveness.

I once heard of a man in England who, because of circumstances, had his sisters-in-law living with him. He was a very godly man. However, his sisters-in-law were teenagers and very worldly. He used to grumble and complain about them all the time. They would go off to dances and parties and he would criticize and condemn them.

One day God spoke to his heart and he realized that he needed to *forgive* them. He had been holding grudges and resentment toward them. He prayed, "God, I do forgive them."

God spoke to his heart saying, "If you really do forgive them, meet them at the railroad station and take umbrellas and galoshes because it is pouring rain there."

This man walked about a mile to the railroad station and stood there waiting in the pouring rain for the train to arrive. When he saw the two girls he said, "I have brought your umbrellas and galoshes and I am here to walk you home."

They were so impressed that they gave their lives to Jesus!

Chapter Four

FORGIVENESS IN MY OWN FAMILY

I found that forgiveness not only works in other families, but in my own as well. *"Judge not, and ye shall not be judged: condemn not, and ye shall not be condemned: forgive, and ye shall be forgiven . . ." (Luke 6:37).*

The Holy Spirit nudged me and said, "How about your sister, Becca?"

Rebecca had always been a fun-loving, carefree girl. As she hit her teen years, rebellion had set in and she got in with the wrong crowd.

She had had a disastrous marriage which ended in divorce and she was now living a wild life away from the Lord. Our mom and dad raised us in a Christian home and always tried to teach us the right way. I had condemned and judged Becca for the way she was living.

Through the revelation of the Holy Spirit, I knew that I had put her in bondage by my actions. That night I prayed the prayer of forgiveness and released her, vowing never again to condemn or judge her.

That very night Becca called us long distance from Indiana. She was crying and wanted to get right with God. She repented, turned toward the pathway of the Lord and is now walking in that light. Praise God!

Forgiveness really does work!

The truth of forgiveness is changing lives all around us. The real clincher for me came when I was released from bondage due to another's forgiveness.

All my life I have had a bad temper. I justified it because my grandfather had one and so did my father. I figured it ran in the family. Since Phyllis and I were married it seemed to be worse than before.

For a long time I did not know that I needed deliverance from that bad temper. When the Lord revealed my need for deliverance, I accepted it! However, that did not completely settle the issue.

I prayed, I rebuked the devil, I was filled with the Holy Spirit, and I still got mad. I did everything I knew I was supposed to do and *nothing* helped.

Finally I came to the place where it was an immovable mountain. I prayed, "Lord, I have tried in the flesh and I've tried in every way that I've seen in your word. Now you are going to have to do something. I have promised Phyllis that I will not get mad and come home to 'let off steam'. I cannot keep that promise unless something happens."

Then one day my answer came! Phyllis came to me and said, "Gene, the Lord spoke to me that I've judged you about your temper and I've been wrong. I want to forgive you for your temper and I want to ask you to forgive me for judging you."

I told her she didn't need to ask for forgiveness because I understood why she would be upset at me.

"It doesn't matter why I felt that way," she continued, "I'm to forgive you!"

I haven't lost my temper since!

FORGIVENESS FREES!

Wives, there are many of you praying condemnation down on your husbands. Husbands, there are many of you doing the same thing to your wives. There are lots of Christians praying condemnation upon their pastors.

You can also bring condemnation upon yourself because you have never seen Jesus in yourself. You say,
"Oh, what a worm I am. What a mess I am. I'm so un-
worthy."

You need to start seeing Jesus *alive* and start making
that confession with your mouth. Jesus is alive *in you!*
Don't get excited about what you are in the flesh, but get
excited about what Jesus is in *you.*

Many people spend thousands of dollars to develop
self-confidence, and still end up in failure. If your confidence is in yourself, it will not be long until you are
shipwrecked. Probably every book that has been written
about men with great self-confidence has an ending that
speaks otherwise. Many of these so-called great men have
either died in prison and the state buried them or they
died paupers. The devil never lets you see the ending
when he tells you how great you are.

The truth is that it is only a matter of letting Christ
come alive in you. Alive *in you!* His way of coming alive
IN US and his words coming forth *FROM US* is his life
being lived *THROUGH US.*

Stephen Strang wrote the introduction to this book.
He told of God's revelation of forgiveness to him. His
wife, Joy, also experienced her own revelation. This was
condemnation on herself.

Joy had had a weight problem since the birth of their
first son. She had tried all the diets available and still
experienced only limited success. Suddenly the words
"forgive yourself" flooded her mind as I was speaking on
the subject of forgiveness.

She said, "Brother Gene, as you said those words, I
suddenly understood my problem. At that very moment I
had a piece of candy in my mouth and as I prayed and
forgave myself, I felt a release inside me."

I could tell from the way she talked she had been
deeply touched by the experience.

She continued, "That candy in my mouth turned so bitter that I had to spit it out. Never again have I had the unsatiable craving for sweets that I once had."

As Joy forgave herself, the condemnation on her lifted. If you can't see Jesus in *yourself*, you can bring condemnation down upon yourself! Until you see Jesus in *yourself*, you will never see *him* in anybody else!

Not long ago I was ministering in a small home prayer group. A precious Christian lady came forward for prayer. Through the gift of word of knowledge, God showed me that her problem was *unforgiveness* and I saw that it all stemmed from something she had done in the past.

"Have you ever considered committing suicide?" I asked.

"Who told you?" she quickly interjected with worry creasing her forehead. "Nobody knew about that. I have never told a living soul."

"God knew," I answered quietly.

As we were talking, our voices were so low that no one else in the group could hear. I could see that she was deeply moved and ashamed for what she had thought and done during her younger years of life. The devil had kept bringing it back to her and the unforgiveness of herself was eating at her very being.

I prayed for her and she smiled and went back to her seat, still not quite sure what had happened. It was two months later before she shared the complete story of what had happened.

"I had asked for the baptism of the Holy Spirit but could not receive due to some blockage," she related. "When you prayed for me that night I forgave myself, even though I didn't quite understand what it meant, and my life changed from that time forward.

"The next week I was vacuuming my house and praising the Lord as I worked. The more I worked, the more I praised, and the more I praised, the more complete I became. Finally I stopped, raised my hands, and started speaking in a beautiful prayer language, just between my Heavenly Father and me. What a release! What a joy! Praise God!

"I am a 'Pink Lady' at the local hospital and the very next week I found that now I had the power to pray for people for whom I had compassion but for whom I formerly could do nothing to help."

She was really excited over all that had come to pass, just because she had forgiven herself!

As you see Jesus in yourself, forgive yourself. As you forgive yourself, peace and contentment will settle upon you. As you are loosed through your own forgiveness, the loosing of bondage is felt deep within yourself.

In Matthew 18:34, Jesus says that if we do not forgive from our hearts, we will be in torment (delivered to the tormentors). Therefore, if we do forgive, there is a release from torment. This also includes forgiving yourself.

A lady was in the prayer room of the church one Sunday morning, waiting patiently for someone to come and help her. She was seeking God, praying with all her heart. She felt that she was in need of deliverance.

I could agree with that! If anyone ever needed deliverance, she did. I could see the torment that was upon her. Surprisingly enough, though, prayer for deliverance did nothing for her. As we talked it seemed that she had forgiven everyone except herself.

She could not forget the past and the things she had done. Finally she said, "Because of Jesus Christ, I forgive myself."

When we don't forgive ourselves, we are coming to the Lord with our own works of righteousness and they are as filthy rags. If we don't accept forgiveness for ourselves, we are trying to get to the Lord on our good deeds!

At this point she saw that Jesus had forgiven her and his blood was sufficient to cleanse her. That is when she received her deliverance. That is when she was released from torment.

I also believe you will not be able to keep your deliverance if there is someone that you have not forgiven. The perfect circle of God's love will be broken and the enemy will flood in upon you.

There was a minister who had a movement against him to remove him from his position. This move was unfair but it gained support until it was successful. He did beautifully against all odds for about two months. Things began to change for the better and God began to take care of his problems. It looked as if the defeat was turning into victory.

But somewhere along the way he let a little root of resentment creep into his heart. It grew and grew. Resentment turned to bitterness, bitterness to rebellion, and finally he lost his ministry. Now he never attends church. He drinks and has many other problems.

If he had only known about forgiveness! Had he forgiven, things would have turned out differently.

FORGIVENESS IS A DECISION. Many people have been very deeply hurt. Many of us think we could forgive if we had someone else's problems, but we cannot forgive with our own problems.

We complicate this by saying, "How can I forgive?" The Lord tells us to love one another. How can we do that? Forget about all the complications and *do* it!

I know a lady who was almost forced off the road recently by another driver. She had a perfect right to be where she was but he drifted over into her lane and was forcing her car off the road. He almost caused her to have an accident.

This man evidently had his own problems. The lady said at first she wanted to chase him down and show him that she had a legal right to be in the lane she was in. Suddenly she realized that she was not going to let this man upset her just because of his problem.

Then she said, "Lord, I love him and I forgive him!"

She began to search for something in the situation to praise the Lord for. Then she found it!

"Thank you, Lord, that I am not married to him!" she almost shouted.

We meet people all through life whom we have to love and forgive. Make up your mind to do it for your own sake as well as for theirs. Say out loud, "Lord, I love them and I forgive them." In this way you are released and they are released as well.

It is time we started loosing people!

That old drunk may always be a drunk if we condemn him for it.

Not only should we not do anything to bind him in alcoholism, but we should work to rescue him. When the disciples rowed against the wind on the Sea of Galilee, they never made shore, but when Jesus came they were immediately on shore — they got there when God's laws worked for them. When we follow God's laws of forgiving we work with him, but when we row against the wind, against God's laws by judging and condemning, we hold back the salvation and redemption of those we judge and condemn, especially, if the person knows of our unforgiveness and sees our reactions and attitudes.

When we start seeing Jesus in ourselves, we can start looking through Jesus' eyes. Do you know what Jesus sees in that old drunk?

He sees a soul! He sees a soul that is worth more than the whole world. The word says that you can gain the whole world and lose your soul and you profit nothing.

As long as we keep condemnation on that person, he will never be set free. That man in the bar knows he is messed up. He doesn't need you to tell him. He is looking to be led out of that darkness into the marvelous light. It takes light to lead them out, not more condemnation.

Jesus said to come on along because there is a new way for you. There is a new kingdom for you! There is a new life for you!

The world needs help! The world doesn't need to be judged! THEY NEED TO HEAR ABOUT JESUS!

If you try to help the world in your power and your strength you will be a failure. Jesus said,

> *If any man hear my words, and believe*
> *not, I judge him not: for I came not to*
> *judge the world, but to save the world.*
> *(John 12:47)*

If we will get the attitude that Christ has and get down off our seats that were occupied by the Pharisees (seats of judgment), quit judging, quit condemning, and start *forgiving,* amazing things will happen!

Chapter Five

FORGIVENESS IN THE CAYMAN ISLANDS

My first trip to the Cayman Islands came about in a very unusual way. I had scheduled two weeks off at Thanksgiving in 1975. I had planned to spend this time with my family. My parents had come to Florida to spend the winter, away from the cold and snow of the Indiana countryside.

We had been ministering throughout the year in various cities around the United States. At this particular time we were ministering in Bryan, Texas. We were looking forward to that two-week vacation with anticipation.

While we were there, my secretary called to ask if it would be possible for me to go to the Cayman Islands. We had been asked to fill in, in place of another ministry, which had to cancel this part of their schedule.

"I'll have to pray about it and see what God would have me do," I said. I thought about my vacation time with my family and at that point I did not want to go to Cayman, wherever it was.

I was never an outstanding geography student when I was in school and I sure didn't know where the *Canary* Islands were. (I had misunderstood my secretary and thought she said Canary Islands.) I figured they were somewhere about mid-ocean in the Pacific, and try as I would, I couldn't remember just where they were, how big, or who owned them or anything concerning them.

These thoughts had rushed through my mind in a flash and then God spoke to me saying, *"Go."* My secretary was still talking, filling me in on some details of the office in Orlando.

"Tell the people I will go," I shouted on the phone. She was surprised at such a quick answer and said, "Are you sure it's all right?"

"Yes, I'm sure!"

"Remember, your mother and father are here from Indiana," she continued. "You won't get to spend that time with them."

I replied, "I understand. God has said I am to go and I've got to do what he wants!"

After the phone conversation was over I began to get excited. I had never ministered in another country. I wondered if the people there spoke English or French or some other language. I could hardly wait to get on my way.

I arrived in Orlando within a couple of days and found that all the arrangements had been made. My secretary handed me my plane tickets amid all the bustle and excitement of greeting the family and trying to get a two-weeks' visit crowded into one day.

The next morning, when I boarded the plane in Miami, I settled down for a long plane ride. I had not even had time to check the schedule and had no idea how far I was to travel or how long it would take. At any rate, I supposed it would take several hours to reach the *Canary* Islands.

After taking off we climbed sharply for a few minutes and the pilot came on the intercom announcing, "We are now over Cuba." I looked out the window and said, "Cuba? What are we doing over Cuba?"

The stewardness smiled and said, "Cuba is between Miami and the Cayman Islands."

"The *Cayman* Islands!" I exclaimed. I pulled out my ticket stub and for the first time looked at my destination. It read, "Grand Cayman." So that's where I was going!

"Just where are the Cayman Islands?" I asked the stewardness.

"They're south of Cuba," she answered. "We will be there in less than an hour."

I didn't know what to expect when I got there. Another person had been scheduled to go with me but plans had to be changed at the last minute. When I arrived in Grand Cayman there were several people standing at the detaining fence, waving to me. They had been told the clothes I would be wearing and therefore recognized me. I had never seen any of these people before. They spoke English but it was the "Queen's English" and my own particular brand of English was almost a foreign language to them.

That night we had a meeting in one of the homes of the people who had met me at the airport. There was much disunity and strife among the group. Most of them were filled with God's Spirit but there was bitterness and resentment and unforgiveness among them.

One couple in particular stood out in my mind because they seemed to have no relationship between each other. Jerry and Paula were Spirit-filled Catholics whom I came to know quite well in the ensuing days.

Revival came to the church at Cayman because the church, which is the body of Christ, began to come together in unity!

God poured out his Spirit in a marvelous way. Literally hundreds were saved, healed, and filled with the Holy Spirit. Because of the witchcraft on the islands, there was also a need for deliverance. God didn't disappoint them in that area either.

Jerry and Paula had spoken to me slightly about their problems. The Lord had revealed a lot about them to me, including the fact that he wanted to heal their marriage.

The last night of the revival I prayed for just that! There was a great move of God that night and almost everyone was going out under the power of God. When I prayed for Jerry, he went under the power and began to laugh. (Paula later told me that it had been years since Jerry had been able to laugh freely.) He received a great deal of deliverance that night.

We ministered to Paula in another room as she began to unravel the story of their 32 years of marriage – the hurts, the disappointments, the resentment, and the accumulation of unforgiveness. I understood the importance of forgiveness in receiving one's own healing but I did not understand at that time that it also loosed others. Paula had such an agonizing tale of woe, but even as she told it she was receiving deliverance! She began to forgive.

The power of God was upon them both.

Later I received this testimony from Jerry concerning their marriage:

"We stayed together, although at times it was not easy. We did not know the Lord and when you do things in the flesh, you reap the flesh; consequently our marriage was a disaster.

"After we came to know the Lord, Paula had an operation which left her cold and indifferent to the fulfilling of her marital obligations of a personal nature. This was a strain on me and a strain on our marriage. The Lord had delivered me from smoking and drinking so I asked him to remove my sexual desires also. He did and I was thankful! I was happy with things the way they were.

"The night Gene prayed for us and our marriage, things began to change. I *forgave Paula* for any feelings of resentment I had for her and she *forgave* me. That very night Paula had promised the Lord that she would do her part in fulfilling our marraige. She did not know how this was going to come about as I no longer had any desire for her.

"The next morning she was depressed. I knew this and prayed with her. I prayed that Jesus would match my sexual desires with hers. I didn't see how anything could happen. As the day went on, Paula prayed for the Lord to show her what to do.

"That night as we were getting ready for bed, we knelt to have prayer together. As I prayed, the Spirit of the Lord came over Paula so strong that she was 'slain in the Spirit'. As she lay on the floor she began to laugh and laugh. I ignored her and continued praying, thinking to myself, that this would never happen to me. Suddenly I too was face down on the bed, laughing and laughing, in the joy of the Lord.

The Lord had ministered to us both and now Paula could see what to do. I walked over to the window as she got into bed.

"Paula said, 'Don't you think we should honor the Lord by doing what he wants us to do?'

"For the first time in over a year I felt a desire for my wife again. Praise the Lord! He beautifully healed our marriage after 32 years.

"This was the first time in our lives that we were man and wife together as the Almighty God planned it. It was beautiful and holy. This was obviously the way God had intended husbands and wives to be. You are not only one in the flesh, you are also one in spirit. In that state God can work through both of you to mature you to his perfect plan for your lives."

What a testimony!

This had been a marriage in name only, but God completely healed it through the power of forgiveness!

Paula and Jerry now have a beautiful deliverance ministry in Cayman. The Lord has also given them a ministry of helps to one another. Paula is now the secretary of the Love of Jesus Ministries of Cayman and Jerry is the treasurer.

God is putting together his body in Cayman and it is based on love and a flowing together with his Spirit.

Chapter Six

PROSPERITY THROUGH FORGIVENESS

What is the will of the Lord? Do we need to perform the will of the Lord? Many times Christians miss it. Are you missing it?

These questions can be resolved by reading the Bible. The Bible is the last will and testament of the Lord Jesus Christ. Resolve these questions, then walk in the pathway God has ordained for you and your life will never be the same. God wills it so!

We discover in the Bible that our legal rights and inheritance are spelled out. Most people are worried about inflation, deflation, recession and depression. It keeps them shook up most of the time, but the answer is simple.

The Lord has already provided answers for all the problems of Christians. All you have to do is be saved and his promise to you is that he is going to take care of you. In the Old Testament it says that God has *all* the silver and gold in the world and the cattle on a thousand hills (See Haggai 2:8; Psalms 50:10). If God is your Father, then by inheritance, your bank account is in good standing.

The Bible tells us that the riches of the ungodly are stored up for the godly. It is time Christians started *knowing* that and *believing* it.

We are told in the Bible that as Christians there are some things *we* are to do. In Matthew, the Lord said to clothe the naked, feed the hungry, and give to those that do not have. How can we do this unless we are prosperous?

If you read in the Old Testament you will find that God had the richest people in the world at that time. I do not believe it is any different in these end times. I can testify as to why I believe that. I see businesses which have been given to God profit unbelievably, while others not given to God are failing.

I can hardly believe what is happening to a Christian brother in Arizona. He sells model homes and is in an area where many companies are going broke. Do you know what he does on Sundays? He closes the door and goes to church and worships the Lord. In return the Lord is blessing him. Competitors say it cannot be done. But, look at the results!

One of the fastest growing chain of restaurants in the country today is in the western states. As you walk in the first thing you see is a sign that says: "We are closed on Sunday so our employees can worship at the church of their choice."

Any businessman will tell you that you do not close a restaurant like that on Sunday. You would go broke! It is amazing!

The Lord is prospering them!

It doesn't make sense to the mind, but it works! Prosperity in the Lord is like that. It never makes sense to the mind, but it works!

If you are planning to sit down with a pencil and paper and figure out the Lord's way to prosperity, just forget it. It doesn't work that way. God is spirit. The Bible and God's ways are not something you can put a pencil to.

You do not have to understand it. If we do understand it, then we make God the same size as our brain and I know that he would be a mighty little God if he was no larger than that. I simply accept the fact that I can never take in the vast expanse of God.

Jesus said, *"Peace I leave with you, my peace I give unto you: not as the world giveth, give I unto you . . ."* *(John 14:27).* We read in Isaiah 53 that the chastisement of our peace was upon him.

That is the reason that Christians who are worried about money need to understand this principle of God. If you are worried about anything, just run the devil off, shout the name of Jesus at him and then lean back in the Lord's arms.

What is prosperity anyway? To people of the world, prosperity is that time between the last installment payment and the next down payment. Also I've heard it said that running into debt isn't embarrassing; it is running into creditors that is embarrassing.

Do you know for sure that God wants to bless you? Do you know that he wants to prosper you? He surely must, for he came down from heaven among all his riches, and he became poor that you might become rich (See II Corinthians 8:9).

I have heard some people say that this scripture was referring merely to spiritual blessings, not money. Paul was talking about money all the way through this chapter and, therefore, this too must have been about money. Actually it was about prosperity.

I was given a quote many years ago that still sticks onto the gummy side of my memory: "The road to success runs uphill, so don't expect to break any speed records." I decided to see just what the Bible said about success. I found only one reference in the King James version to success and that was in Joshua 1:8:

> *This book of the law shall not depart out*
> *of thy mouth; but thou shalt meditate*
> *therein day and night, that thou mayest*
> *observe to do according to all that is*
> *written therein: for then thou shalt make*

> *thy way prosperous, and then thou shalt*
> *have good success.*

It is time that Christians started battling the devil for their rightful inheritance! The Lord paid for it but we have to be the battleground — we must yield to the works of Jesus. Up until now, most of us have given away our inherited rights. *By our mouth* we have given it to the devil; we spend all too much time binding and rebuking Satan. We would do better to talk to Jesus and ask him to POUR ON MORE ANOINTING!

A song we sing a lot says, "I want a cabin in the corner of Glory Land." If you have just a cabin, then you missed Glory! The Bible says you are going to have a *mansion* . . . not a cabin. We need to recognize the rights and privileges God has provided for us.

I heard a man say the other day that he wanted to get a glimpse of Jesus in eternity. I want more than a glimpse! The Bible says we will be forever in his presence. The sinner will get a glimpse at the judgment. I do not want a glimpse, I want to be there forever. Hallelujah!

The devil has told Christians for the past 2,000 years that the more patches they had on their pants, the more spiritual they were. That is not true and God certainly does not want you to be miserable on earth. We can find our answer in the word and it can bring peace to your mind and rest to your heart.

This message had rung true to a couple we are closely related to in the Lord in Orlando. Frank and Charlotte had attended our prayer group during their courtship days and it was our privilege to join them in holy matrimony. They were extremely happy and dedicated to the Lord's work, but prosperity seemed to elude them.

A few months ago they had reached their financial end. Their faith had begun to waver concerning financial prosperity.

George and Mary Jo sat down with them and began to recite the promises of God from the Bible.

"I know all that," Charlotte interjected. "It just doesn't seem to work in our case. What's wrong?"

Frank agreed. "I feel we have done everything we can find in the word and still our financial situation is getting worse and worse."

The four prayed together and decided that on Thursday night they would meet at the home of Frank and Charlotte. Frank was told to bring out his records and bring all his current bills up to date until it could be seen just what financial shape they were in.

The next Thursday the four sat at the dining room table, looked at the financial picture and sure enough, it was bad. They had bills for gasoline credit cards from various companies, Master Charge, BankAmericard drugstore charge account, clothing stores charge accounts, back payments on two houses (one that each of them had before their marriage), loan company notes, etc. The pile was an immovable mountain, but they sorted through, added it and it amounted to more than $9,000.00.

They laid hands on the pile of bills, their billfolds and checkbooks, joined together in prayer, submitted the whole thing to the Lord, rebuked the devil, and thanked the Lord for supplying the need. Then they said, "Pour on more anointing, Lord!"

They went through the house, stopping in each room to pray, and asked to the Lord to correct all wrongs in the household. They stopped at the power meter outside, because their power bills were also exorbitant, and asked the Lord to take all waste and allow only the amount necessary to flow through the meter for their entire needs.

As they returned into the dining room, Mary Jo received a word of knowledge and said, "I feel there is some unforgiveness in Charlotte."

Charlotte agreed. She still held resentment against her ex-husband and had not completely forgiven him.

At the time of the divorce she was left with two children and all the bills. She was a music director and member of quite a large church in another denomination. She was one of the few female music directors of a church of this size and made a nice salary. Her entire training and all her college preparation was in this field and she was well qualified for this particular position.

She knew that denomination would not use a music director who was divorced, so she resigned rather than be terminated. Now she had no way to support her two children and had been unable to find a job for some time. When she eventually did get a job, it was teaching in a public school where she had little experience and consequently drew a proportionately small salary. Her living standard took tremendous strides downward.

After she shared this, she was told that it did not matter whose fault it was, forgiveness was necessary to have victory in her life. She was told that as you forgive, so your Father in heaven forgives you. She forgave him and all the other people who had ever hurt her in any way. Again they prayed and Frank joined in with his own turn at forgiveness.

The very next week miracles started to happen. Creditors who previously were calling often and threatening to sue, suddenly became nice and seemed to change their whole attitude about them. It had been decided that Frank would call each and every one of the past-due creditors and tell them they were working on a solution to settle the account. Each call helped to build his faith because each time they thanked him for calling and told him they would wait for the money owed them. What a reversal to what he was used to!

The house they were no longer living in was standing empty, and though payments had been made on it, they were falling behind on the payments on the house they were living in. Then a miracle happened! A man became interested in buying the empty house, and less than a month later closed the deal, giving them more money than they had expected. Praise God!

Five weeks from the time they prayed for forgiveness, Frank went to their regular Friday night fellowship meeting. He was so excited he could hardly contain himself.

He had agreed that each month he would add up how much was still owed and actually witness how God was bringing him out of poverty into prosperity. That past week when he added it up he found that almost three thousand dollars had been lopped off the top of the bill. There was only a little over six thousand dollars left to pay.

"How did it happen?" he was asked.

"I don't know. I'm like the blind man that Jesus healed who said, *'all I know is that once I was blind and now I see!'* That is my testimony. Once I was deeply in debt, but now PROSPERITY is coming to my home. Praise the Lord!"

Frank and Charlotte have continued to move in this direction. As they pay off each debt, they trust more fully in their supplier, the Lord Jesus Christ. They have destroyed their charge cards and each day God supplies their every need!

They have truly found the answer, just as it was given in Joshua 1:8. They have observed to do all that is written and their way is prosperous and they are having good success.

Still, after all this, Charlotte and Frank were not completely free on forgiveness. A few weeks after this, Charlotte attended a music festival. On the way there that morning she was quoting scripture and praising the Lord as she drove along. The last scripture she quoted before arriving was the Lord's Prayer, and it seemed to really speak to her as she said, "forgive me."

When she arrived at the festival, a young lady approached her with recognition and greeted her warmly. Though she had grown up since Charlotte's days as church music director, she was remembered.

She had once told her mother, "When I grow up I want to be just like Miss Charlotte, a church music director."

As soon as Charlotte saw the young lady, these memories started flooding back upon her. Satan immediately began to saddle her with a guilt feeling because of the things that had happened in her life. Though she could not help what had happened, and though the Lord had completely forgiven her, she had not completely forgiven herself and therefore the devil started to jump in.

As soon as she could gracefully excuse herself from the young lady, she did so. Her day was ruined. She left the festival and went toward home, literally crushed!

After she got home, she was too ashamed to tell her husband, so it was several hours until she could finally get it out. He immediately realized what was wrong and suggested she should say the Lord's Prayer with sincerity and emphasis on "forgive us." As she said it, she really forgave herself as Jesus forgave her!

God had given her the answer that very morning before she got there and she had failed to recognize it.

Frank realized the full significance of forgiveness and though he had forgiven his former wife already, he had never told her so and therefore had not completely released her. He sat down, wrote her a letter and told her he forgave her for everything and asked that she also forgive him.

He later talked with the pastor of her church by long distance telephone and was informed she had been in church, and was also receiving the benefits of forgiveness.

THE POWER OF FORGIVENESS GOES ON AND ON!

> *Wherein in time past ye walked according to the course of this world, according to the prince of the power of the air, the spirit that now worketh in the children of disobedience: (Eph. 2:2).*

Remember that Satan is entitled to exert influence on any area of our life that is in disobedience. The key to prosperity for Frank and Charlotte was obedience in forgiveness. They were already walking in the light in all the other aspects of prosperity and then the truth in forgiveness came forth to complete the manifestation of prosperity and success.

Chapter Seven

FORGIVENESS HEALS
MARRIAGE PROBLEMS

Husbands, love your wives, even as Christ
also loved the church, and gave himself
for it; (Ephesians 5:25).

Do you know that one of the strongest powers in the
world is a husband and wife united in prayer (if the home
is in spiritual order)? Do you know that is why the devil
hates for homes to get in the order that God ordained
them?

The devil will do everything within his power to break
up the home unity!

Modern America has a multitude of broken marriages
due to the influence of Satan. These broken marriages are
the breeding ground of the biggest area of unforgiveness
among Christians today. Forgiveness is a two-way benefit.
If we do not forgive others, we ourselves are not forgiven
by God.

Frank and Charlotte blocked prosperity in their lives
because of their collective unforgiveness. Charlotte forgave completely the night at their home when they
prayed together. It was a few weeks later when Frank
completely forgave his ex-wife for all the problems in
their lives. Forgiveness also healed many other problems
in this marriage.

A classical example of unforgiveness came about in the spring of 1974. I had received my healing from multiple sclerosis and diabetes in December, 1973. We were ministering each Friday night in a prayer group in Orlando and the Lord was blessing us mightily.

One Friday afternoon in early April I was on my way home to get ready to go to the prayer group. I decided on the spur of the moment to stop at a roadside fruit stand to get some tomatoes.

As I was sorting through the tomatoes, the lady beside me was singing softly, "Jesus On The Main Line."

I looked at her and grinned, "You must be a Holy Roller!"

"I love Jesus and am proud of it," she replied.

"Praise the Lord," was my response and we both knew we had formed a friendship.

This was my introduction to Mary Jo, the lady who was later to become my administrative assistant at Love of Jesus Ministries. Her husband, George, was with her and we talked for perhaps five minutes. I told them of the prayer group that met at the apartment complex and invited them to come. They didn't get there that night but the following week they came.

I knew nothing about them at that time except what I had seen at the fruit market. They seemed happy and devoted to each other. Near the end of the meeting, when we gave the call for anyone who needed prayer, they came together. God showed me that they both harbored unforgiveness.

I talked first with Mary Jo. "Who do you hold resentment toward?" I asked. "Who have you not forgiven?"

Her eyes sparked with anger. "I'm not resentful!" She fairly spit it out. (She later told me that she was so angry at that moment she could have struck me.)

I waited for her to say more for I knew there was more she needed to say. Perhaps a minute went by and her defiant head started to drop. I could see that the Holy Spirit was doing a work in her.

"I must not have forgiven everyone or I would not have gotten mad when you asked that question," she reasoned.

"Who have you not forgiven?" I gently asked her again.

"My ex-husband, I suppose," she answered. "I thought I had forgiven him for all the hurt that was caused during our separation and divorce. I must not have or I wouldn't feel all this anger and confusion."

Later we talked over this whole experience and she said she had no idea she still held resentment for him until I asked her that question. She was surprised at how mad she became when I asked her. She had forgiven him in her mind but had never said so out loud, so the forgiveness was not complete. It is important that we confess our sins.

I talked with her for a few moments and directed her to ask forgiveness and confess it as a sin. Hot tears flooded down her face as she did.

I turned to George and said, "Who do you have to forgive?"

"My ex-wife, " was his answer.

Both of them had thought they had forgiven their previous mates. Both of them had much the same story. They had tried to live their lives the way of the world and Satan had played havoc with them. They had both been saved and baptized together after their marriage. In fact, Mary Jo's two children had been saved at the same time she was, so the baptismal service was a family affair.

I then had the two of them join hands and I laid hands on them, prayed a forgiveness prayer over them, asking God to remove all hurts, and to fill all voids with the love of Jesus. They both went under the power at the same time and fell flat on their backs, still tightly holding hands!

From that very moment a relationship was born through the power of the Holy Spirit that has never

diminished. God brought about this meeting just as he
leads us in all things, for the Bible says that those that are
born of the Spirit are led by the Spirit.

God did a mighty work in the lives of George and Mary
Jo that night. True forgiveness brought about a whole-
someness to their lives. Mary Jo's two children began to
respond better to their new home environment. Bible
study at home brought about a new awareness of God
and his blessings.

George's three children (all of whom were married and
had a home of their own) could see a difference in the
relationship of George and Mary Jo. The older daughter
and her husband were saved, then a few months later the
younger daughter and her husband accepted Jesus.
Finally the son and his wife were welcomed into the
family of God by the rest of the family.

Forgiveness really works!

As each member of the family was saved, each one in
turn received the gift of the baptism in the Holy Spirit.
Today when this family gets together it's a hallelujah
time!

You always have a choice whether you want to forgive
or not.

FORGIVENESS IS A DECISION.

Unforgiveness is a sin.

Psalms 66:18 says that if I regard iniquity in my heart,
God doesn't even hear me. There is no need for me to go
to the altar to pray when my prayers are not heard. So
many of God's children are not getting prayers answered
and have lost the peace of God that they once had. Is it
because they have iniquity in their hearts?

I know a Christian woman who did not want to see her
daughter get married. Neither of the girl's parents were in
favor of the marriage. Finally, the daughter ran away
from home and got married anyway. As a result, her
mother was filled with sorrow, despair, and bitterness.
She was in a very bad state. She could not find any peace
of mind.

One day at noontime she went into a church to pray and seek the Lord. As she sat there, God spoke to her with these words, "You do not lose your peace with God over someone else's sin – only over your own."

As she heard God speak, a great cleansing came over her. She felt relief as she said, "I forgive my daughter and I forgive my new son-in-law." They were the ones in the wrong. But as the mother forgave them, she received this release and the peace of God flooded back into her life. She also was wrong in not being willing to forgive.

Forgiveness is an attribute of God. He longs to forgive. It does not matter how bad our sins are. It does not matter how rebellious we may have been. When we ask his forgiveness he puts only one limitation on us – we first must forgive others their trespasses.

A lady in our church came to the pastor's wife and said she needed help. She was the picture of dejection. She said, "I have lost my joy. I have no joy and I am under constant Satanic attack."

In talking with her, the Spirit of the Lord directed the pastor's wife to realize there were people in her life whom she had not forgiven. One was her husband, one was her mother-in-law.

"Do you forgive your husband?" she was asked.

"I understand how he feels," was the reply.

She was dodging the question. The same thing happened with questions about her mother-in-law.

She was asked to say *out loud* that she would forgive these people to the best of her ability and with the Lord's help. When she tried to say it, she couldn't. Then she realized that forgiving was harder than she had thought. This was her problem.

As prayer was given, she finally had real victory. She forgave her husband and her mother-in-law by an act of her will, and release followed immediately.

The amount of pardon or forgiveness we receive from God is totally dependent upon whether or not we have forgiven others. When we harbor resentment, hurts, hostility, or hatred, and do not forgive our brother, we are leaving the door open for Satan to attack. We must walk in the light of forgiveness. It may be the hardest thing you have ever done, but God says . . . *forgive!*

Forgiveness is a *decision*, not an *emotion.*

Emotions can be good. God made our emotions but we cannot live on our emotions. We must live on our decisions. Surrendering your life to Jesus Christ may have included an emotional experience for you, but it was the decision that made the changes.

Chapter Eight

A YEAR OF HEALING AND FORGIVENESS

The story told in this chapter is God's healing of a marriage. After nine years, their marriage had come to an end. Then they decided to trust in the power of Almighty God to restore it.

I asked Maria to tell her story and the following is an account of how God restored the years to them through forgiveness.

The lesson is plain. Too many people cannot forgive themselves. Be able to forgive yourself or Satan will have a field day with you. God will forgive you the first time you ask. You do not have to be in torment over anything. *"If we confess our sins, he is faithful and just to forgive us our sins . . ." (I John 1:9).* Don't let Satan keep you under condemnation.

Lee and Maria were both Catholic; both raised in the church, but both with a minimum commitment to God. Lee was 11 years older than Maria and when they decided to get married, Maria's parents were dead set against it. Lee was in the Air Force and Maria was busy putting herself through college until Lee appeared on the scene. They were determined to marry so when the parents objected, they eloped.

They had what they called a *contract marriage,* meaning they felt free to break it without regrets. After their son was born, Lee felt inclined to test it on several occasions. He was unable to decide between marriage and being a bachelor.

Maria, being a prideful young lady, tried hard to keep these things hidden from everyone. Finally she found that her supposedly "well-kept secret" wasn't so secret. Her confidant and friend turned out to be one of his admirers. Her family also felt that she was putting on a show of everything being rosy when it was anything else but rosy.

Maria tried to play all roles at once: mother, father, organizer, bill payer, etc. She seemed happy on the outside but she was a seething hurricane on the inside. Finally she exploded and she and Lee split with such violence that Lee volunteered for counseling. The Lord then began to move in their lives. Maria felt it was the Lord's will that they separate until he could truly unite them as they were meant to be united.

In February, 1976, the Lord started to work on Maria. It seemed that things got worse and then they slowly started to improve. Her daughter was constantly ill, preventing her from working full time. She was unsure whether her husband would continue to provide for her and the children or not. The landlady was pressing her to buy the house they were living in or move out. More and more, fears pressed in on her daily and she had no one to turn to for help. She had moved from another state to Florida and had no friends there and did not form friendships easily.

She constantly told everyone how great things were, while on the inside she was miserable. She needed friends and had none. She needed her family but they couldn't stand her ups and downs. She had left the church because she didn't want to face any condemnation for her planned divorce.

Just when things were at the lowest ebb, hope came in like a bright new ray of sunlight. She was welcomed into a group of separated and divorced Catholics and went to one of their meetings. They encouraged her to again go back to Mass and she did, immediately feeling some relief.

Then several churches of various denominations began a ten-week city-wide crusade with the purpose of bringing people back to Christ. She had no other place to go so she started attending. Slowly she realized the void she had created by denying God and blaming him for the mess her life was in. She began to come alive to the desire of leading a "normal" life, with the father of her children in their own home.

She began to cry out to God to repair her life, to show her how to change it. She cried for weeks, attending a different teaching session every night, gradually learning what Christianity really is. Though she was a Catholic, she had never heard teaching on what made homes and families bond together; what made men truly men, strong, supportive, protective and perhaps most important, dependable. Still she hadn't found what *she* was looking for, and though she was going to Mass on Sunday, it gave her no satisfaction or lasting peace.

One Wednesday just before Easter she was attending a teaching series on *The Living Christ.* The teacher of the session impressed her with his kind, gentle, compassionate ways. He spoke of Jesus as though he knew him personally. The key to this man's life was his one hundred percent commitment to Jesus Christ and a deep desire to obey every law at all times. This was the thing that really spoke to her.

She knew that she had never given one hundred percent to anything, ever, but now she knew she must. At that point she made a *total* commitment to God!

The teacher went on to say that he felt that for anyone to remain a Christian in this day, he *must* belong to a Christian community. She asked about one and was told of a Catholic prayer community which met regularly every Thursday night. Her spirit jumped within her at the thought of again belonging! She knew in her heart that her search for herself was almost over.

She felt an urgency, a sudden expectancy, but for what she didn't know. It took a lot of effort to attend that first meeting, but she made it! On the way she said she felt a burden. She felt like crying and did not know why, and yet another part of her was light and bubbly.

The meeting started with a song and from that point on Maria didn't know too much of what happened. She stood rooted in the back of the room, quietly crying buckets of tears. Her soul was washed clean by tears as she invited Jesus to work a complete overhaul in her life.

After the meeting, some of the group came over to her and asked if she needed prayer.

"Yes!" she blurted out. "Pray for my life! I'm a mess! I need a new start!" Little did she know that the Lord had surely guided her into the pathways in which she was now walking. Jesus was in control of her life!

A sudden peace came over her, a quietness inside, and she did not question it when they had finished praying for her. She accepted the quietness as her answer to her need.

About a week later her younger sister said, "What good thing has happened to you, Maria?"

"What do you mean?"

"For the first time in six months you are smiling. What are you smiling about?"

She didn't have too good an answer for she was all wrapped up in her own thoughts. She fully accepted the fact that changes were taking place in her. She knew that she had shed a tremendous burden.

That was truly Maria's beginning! People say they are "reborn" or "born again" and she felt a rebirth too! For the first time in her life, though she had attended Catholic schools for 12 years, she was beginning to understand the meaning of the cross, salvation, and that Christ died for her!

Suddenly her hunger for God's word began to manifest itself. She didn't have a Bible and found she wanted one badly. Her birthday was in June and her mother asked her what she wanted.

"A Bible," was her instant reply.

The gift was forthcoming and it was a gigantic large print family Bible. She began to read and as she read she saw how short of the mark her life had been until that time. Even though she was learning about God's plan for family life, she was not ready to completely accept it.

She did not want to accept that her marriage vows were binding and that Lee belonged as her husband and father of their children. She was beginning to enjoy life without him. Still she couldn't shake off the feeling that she was not living according to God's plan.

> *Likewise, ye wives, be in subjection to your own husbands; that, if any obey not the word, they also may without the word be won by the conversation of the wives . (I Peter 3:1)*
>
> *The wife hath not power of her own body, but the husband: and likewise also the husband hath not power of his own body, but the wife. (I Corinthians 7:4)*
>
> *Wives, submit yourselves unto your own husbands, as unto the Lord. (Ephesians 5:22)*

These scriptures stayed with her and she argued with herself and God. Then Lee called and said he was coming to Florida in June. She panicked! She didn't trust him! She didn't believe anything he said and most of all, she didn't want him back.

"Maybe he does provide us with most everything materially," she thought, "But he has no rights. It's his duty to pay!" She felt so righteous.

He came anyway and she found that she didn't hate him anymore. But she still didn't trust him! She was surprised that she could talk to him. She felt sorry for him, the children, and herself. They had made a massive mess of their life. It was a relief when he left.

In August she asked to join the group that ministers in song for the prayer community. They first prayed about it and then accepted her. She felt for the first time that she had earned her place in the sun.

Singing had always been an important part of her life, in one form or another: choirs, chorals in college and such. Now she was singing for the Lord and she thanked him for finding a way to use the talents in which she took great pleasure.

As she continued reading the Bible over the next few weeks, the healing process continued. The Lord taught her many things. She learned to deal with her own anger and resentments and begin to forgive instead of festering. She learned to develop self-control of her tongue and temper and acquired patience.

Lee, though he was in another state, was calling weekly, usually just as some financial catastrophe was occurring. She never seemed to be prepared for the emergencies and found she had to rely on him each time. She hated to admit her failures, but began to see that God was showing her how she could and should rely on Lee in areas she had never done before. This admission did not come easy.

She wasn't sure she liked him anymore. She felt she knew for certain she could not love him again as a wife should love her husband. Still, Lee kept telling her that she should (and the Lord was telling her the same thing). Again the passages in the Bible began to convict her. She didn't want to get on a merry-go-round again. As Lee's retirement from the Air Force got closer, she got more and more frantic.

By November she had lost her peace and joy. She was again living with all the old bitterness and anger welling up inside her. She fussed with the kids, shifting her own frustrations to them.

She cried out to the Lord. "All right, I'll be his wife, but you will have to make me feel the part. I can't do it myself. I don't even want to try except that I acknowledge that it is your will. Help me, Lord!"

With this decision, she experienced a quiet peace in her soul and a lightness in her heart once again. She no longer feared or dreaded the day Lee would arrive. A part of her even anticipated his arrival with pleasure, although she was not sure she fully trusted the Lord.

Lee immediately sensed that she was not completely "sold out" when he got there. They both agreed not to tackle their problem until after Christmas and so they shelved everything until after the holidays.

Individually they prayed, asking God to show them where to go for counseling, knowing they could not solve their problems alone. Lee had been well appraised of his personality splits and was learning to control the dominant ones that had no place in the world he wanted: a home with a wife where he could be husband and father. This is as it should be — as God ordained it! Sometimes men forget how to be men, probably because it is so much easier to stay as a child.

Maria could not place much faith in a priest due to past experience. She had also gone to a group therapy clinic for eight weeks prior to leaving Lee. The most that was accomplished was to convince her that she was not the one with the problem and that she was strong enough to stand by herself. Now she understood that both were foolish assumptions.

If she went to a community health center, she knew they could not accept her wanting to reverse the roles of women and men back 2000 years. Neither would they understand her giving total support to a committed marriage until she could see the results. It was like putting the cart before the horse.

Just before Christmas, they both attended the Catholic community prayer meeting where the sign at the entrance read, "Gene Lilly, Evangelist, ministering on forgiveness."

At the end of the teaching on forgiveness, Maria went forward for ministry. She had at one time suffered a whiplash that still, at times, became sore and bothersome. Lee also went forward asking prayer for his heart.

Lee was in front of Maria and Gene had not completed praying when Lee was "slain in the Spirit." He cried for a long time and as he got up he looked amazed.

"I don't know why I've been laying on the floor, but I sure do feel much more free," he said.

Maria was next. Down she went beside Lee. Floods of joy and trust in the greatness of God Almighty swept across her. Forgiveness flowed between them.

Later, Lee and Maria came back asking for prayer for the healing of their marriage. A prayer for forgiveness and a marriage overhaul was given in the mighty name of Jesus.

A few days later, Maria realized that her neck no longer gave her any trouble. Lee had no further problems with his heart. They both no longer considered "if their marriage didn't work" but instead began saying, "now that it is working!"

They had truly given *all* to do the will of the Lord, knowing and believing he would arrange things for their own good.

Now the *Lord* is making the decisions in their lives!

This is not to say they listen all the time or follow even when they have heard. But they quickly see their error, discuss it and correct it. Lee does the correcting of their mistakes and Maria submits to his decision, happy because she knows the source of his decision.

Lee and Maria want their children to be exciting, genuine Christians, brought up in a Christian home, knowing Christ as their personal Saviour. This is something neither of them had while growing up or during the nine years of their marriage.

Forgiveness healed their marriage!

Chapter Nine

FORGIVENESS NECESSARY FOR PHYSICAL HEALING

Many people are asking why their prayers for healing are not being answered. Is it because they aren't forgiving? There is no point in praying if there is something wrong between you and your brother.

A woman I know had prayed many times concerning sickness in her body. She could not get her prayers answered. Finally she came to me for help.

"This arthritis is getting me down," she complained. "I need help badly."

People who have resentment and unforgiveness and hold grudges often have arthritis. That does not mean that everyone who has arthritis has an unforgiving spirit. However, if you do have arthritis it sure won't hurt to check to make sure you are not holding something against someone.

It's possible that someone can break a bone and the devil is so rotten that he will rush in and infect that area with arthritis. Not everyone with arthritis has resentment.

People who criticize and complain about everything and are filled with resentment, and vocalize it constantly, often develop arthritis which settles in the middle knuckle. It often settles in the tips of the fingers of those who silently resent.

The tips of this woman's fingers were seriously gnarled. "Would you pray for me," she asked.

She was asked if she had any resentment in her heart. She replied that she did. She said that ever since she was a teenager, she resented the poverty in which she was raised. She was asked if she could confess that and forgive.

She said yes.

They laid hands on her hands and began to command the arthritis to go in the name of Jesus. Suddenly, she interrupted shouting,

"Look, look!" The knots are going away!"

They watched as swelling in her fingers went down and the knots went away. Her physical healing came through forgiveness as she released resentment. Application of God's laws of forgiveness are as important as his Ten Commandments.

After our pastor's wife finished speaking on the importance of forgiving at a women's meeting, a woman came to her and said she had arthritis very bad in her index finger. The woman said she thought it was caused by pointing an accusing finger at others. It had been swollen and very painful.

"While you were talking, I decided to forgive everybody I could think of," she said.

She had recalled one by one the people she felt she was resentful toward. The arthritis left while she was going through the list. Her finger was completely healed.

HER HEALING CAME THROUGH FORGIVENESS!
Divine healing is a benefit of forgiveness.

We have already dealt with healing of arthritis. We all know how it is to be hurt and we have not felt very forgiving at times. But what are the results? Tension, nerve disorders, tension headaches, colon trouble; all these and many other afflictions can crop up when we want revenge or retaliation. We can develop resentment. Resentment can grow into rebellion. Rebellion can turn into hatred.

Terrible things can enter in when Satan gets a foothold in your life. If you have bad nerves, see if you feel someone is getting the better of you.

James, the brother of Jesus, was writing to the Jews. His book in the Bible is an easy book to understand and maybe we can see a little of ourselves in it. As James is writing this, he refers to the people as his brethren, so he is writing to Christians, or saints of God.

As we look through these five chapters, we find that there were people who despised the poor and elevated the rich. Some of them had faith but not works. Everybody wanted to be the boss. There were double-minded men who would praise the Lord one minute and curse him the next. There was envy and strife and there was earthly wisdom rather than spiritual wisdom. They were greedy, worldly and proud. They never considered the Lord's will but made up their own minds.

James was writing to them to try to correct this situation. He talks about prayer and healing. James 5:14 says:

> *Is any sick among you? let him call for the elders of the church; and let them pray over him, anointing him with oil in the name of the Lord.*

I am sure you have read that before, but that is not the end of it. Verses 15 and 16 say:

> *And the prayer of faith shall save the sick, and the Lord shall raise him up; and if he have committed sins, they shall be forgiven him.*
>
> *Confess your faults one to another, and pray one for another, that ye may be healed . . .*

You may go forward for prayer, have the elders of the church pray for you, anointing you with oil in the name of the Lord, and then go home wondering why you were not healed. You see, there is a connection between healing and confessing faults, getting things put right.

This goes right along with what Jesus said: *"Go and sin no more lest a worse thing come upon you."*

Once when he was going to raise up a man sick with the palsy, Jesus said, *". . . Son, — thy sins be forgiven thee " (Matt. 9:2).* Before this man could have healing, I believe he had to have his sins forgiven.

James, writing to the brethren, said to confess your faults one to another and pray for one another that you may be healed. If you have sins, they shall be forgiven you.

Not long ago on a trip through the western states, we prayed for a man I will identify as W.C. He was suffering with asthma and an extremely bad heart. As we talked with him, he told us the following story.

His mother had been quite wealthy and had given various properties to her sons. She had given an expensive boat to the brother of W.C., and had given him extensive stock holdings in a well-known company for safe-keeping, as well as other financial holdings.

This brother, a widower, married for the second time. He lived with this new wife for a few short years, along with her children by a former marriage.

He became ill and a doctor performed brain surgery on him for a tumor. He did not survive the surgery. His second wife had signed the release papers for the surgery and resentment was harbored by W.C.

Later it was said there had been no brain tumor after all. More resentment built up in W.C.

W.C. felt that the stock holdings should have been returned to his mother, whom he felt was the rightful owner. Instead, the stock was given to the step-children, along with the expensive boat. The boat then was transferred to another man by a legal transaction.

All this had built into an unsurmountable mountain of resentment in W.C. He resented his sister-in-law and felt he could never forgive her.

I shared with him that his healing hinged on forgiveness. He said it seemed to be unforgivable, but then, remembering Jesus who is faithful to forgive, it seemed possible.

We prayed together for complete forgiveness, and then I prayed a prayer for his physical healing.

PRAISE GOD! A MIRACLE HAPPENED! He received a new heart!

Two days later he visited the doctor in the adjoining town. The doctor said his heart sounded good. Then he asked him to check the carotid arteries on each side of his neck, leading from his heart to his brain. The doctor listened through his instrument, but said they were still blocked.

That night W.C. called and asked me to come to his house and again pray for him for those arteries to be clear.

Phyllis and I went by and prayed. His wife asked for us to pray for her to receive the baptism of the Holy Spirit. She received a beautiful prayer language.

About a month later we received a letter from W.C. He filled us in on what had happened since he had truly forgiven his sister-in-law.

"My wife and I were getting ready to leave for church," he wrote. "I had gone upstairs to put on my tie when a shortness of breath suddenly engulfed me. First we prayed in the name of Jesus, and then my wife called my doctor. Another doctor was on call that morning and said he would meet us in an hour at the local hospital emergency room.

"After that my wife called our church office to request prayer, remembering that the scripture tells us to call on the elders of the church to pray for healing.

"In fact, the associate pastor prayed with us on the telephone, then at the morning worship service the congregation joined in prayer for my healing.

"In the meantime I was admitted to the emergency room and underwent tests of blood pressure and blood count, plus chest X-rays. The doctor said he could not understand as he could find nothing wrong with my breathing and all the test results were good."

At that point W.C.'s wife said, "PRAISE THE LORD!" and told the doctor about her husband being prayed for.

"Doctor, will you please listen to my carotid arteries?"

"Of course," he replied.

He listened intently for a few moments and looked up to tell W.C., "They are perfectly clear." At that point all three praised the Lord together, for the doctor was also a born-again Christian.

W.C. and his wife returned home with a new freedom in their spirits, confident that all his health problems were resolved through the power of forgiveness and the name of Jesus.

Often when a person is healed by the power of Almighty God, a battle begins within the person. Satan gets in the door by putting doubt in the mind. God's word is definite about healing and we must rely on it by faith when Satan brings doubt.

At times a demonic presence will try to manifest itself after a healing and the person healed will become aware of a symptom of the former illness. DON'T BELIEVE IT! Rebuke it. SPEAK THE WORD. You either have it or you don't have it!

At the time of each attack of the enemy you have a right to either pray and battle the devil or accept the sickness. The answer is in James 4:7;

"Submit yourself therefore to God. Resist the devil, and he will flee from you."

Each time, you have a choice to confess this powerful promise of God — a choice of submitting yourself to God and resisting the devil — or of submitting yourself to the devil and his symptoms and resisting God. That's why it is so important to continue to read the word and build up your warfare weapons to fight the devil.

W.C. and his wife started to do battle against the enemy the moment the first symptoms came back. *They* prayed! They called the church and the *pastor* prayed! Then the *church congregation* prayed.

The answer came just like it says in James 4:7. They resisted the devil and submitted themselves to God and Satan and his henchmen had to *flee* from them. Praise God!

Since that time we have had contact with them several times. Their lives are now in victory and they praise God for his healing power and his goodness. Forgiveness was the pathway to the power to resist the devil and maintain a healing which came when W.C. forgave.

Chapter Ten

FORGIVENESS BRINGS UNITY

Jesus was talking in Matthew 16:18 when he said, *". . . Upon this rock I will build MY church; and the gates of hell shall not prevail against it."*

Do you suppose that Jesus was talking about a church building? Do you suppose he was talking about a particular denomination? I don't think so.

In Acts 7:38 we read of the church in the wilderness with Moses and the children of Israel. It says God lived in the Tabernacle. Then in the 48th verse it says, *"The most High dwelleth not in temples made with hands . . ."*

Where does God dwell then? In our INNERMOST BE-ING, that's where. In Revelation 3:20 the Bible says:

> *Behold, I stand at the door, and knock: if any man hear my voice, and open the door, I will come in to him, and will sup with him, and he with me.*

When Christ sets out to build his church, it is not a building, but men and women. God chooses to live in us.

Jesus said he would build *his* church. Remember one thing though: if we do not allow him to build it in us, then he won't own it! It must be built his way or it will not stand!

In Ephesians, chapter four, Paul is talking about the unity of the Spirit in the bond of peace. In verse 13 he says:

*"Till we all come in the unity of the faith,
and of the knowledge of the Son of God,
unto a perfect man, unto the measure of
the stature of the fullness of Christ."*

Do you understand what this says? We must come into unity of the faith and knowledge of Jesus, to a mature person, in the likeness of Jesus Christ.

Paul compares the building of the church to regular earthly buildings. He writes of the architect laying the foundation, and of the stones fitting together.

Church order in the New Testament comes when Jesus is the architect. Did you know that you can have an architect draw blueprints of a beautiful building but you can't build that building until you have the necessary material?

What are the materials? The stones to build the church. Who are the stones? You and I. No matter how accurate we are about the blueprints (church order), unless we are the right kind of stones and are willing to be fitted together by the Master Builder, then we cannot construct the building, the Church, the body of Christ.

Psalm 133 says that brethren should dwell together in unity. This is not possible without forgiveness! We need to stop building walls between denominational differences and start building bridges through relationships.

In the First Epistle General of John, chapter one, verse 6 and 7, it says:

*If we say that we have fellowship with
him, and walk in darkness, we lie, and do
not the truth:*

*But if we walk in the light, as he is in
the light, we have fellowship one with
another, and the blood of Jesus Christ his
Son cleanses us from all sin.*

What is walking in darkness? In the second chapter, the 11th verse it says,

*But he that hateth his brother is in dark-
ness, and walketh in darkness, and*

> *knoweth not whither he goeth, because*
> *that darkness hath blinded his eyes.*

If you hate your brother, you don't know where you are going. Things are in confusion. FORGIVE!

Verse 10 says, *"He that loveth his brother abideth in the light, and there is none occasion of stumbling in him."*

God's perfect love is like a completed circle. When we do not forgive, there is a break in the circle, thereby giving place to the devil.

Forgiveness is necessary to bring unity in churches, between one church and the next, and one denomination and the next.

There was a fundamentalist pastor in a city who was intent upon attacking a certain congregation, and specifically their pastor. He would go on his radio broadcast saying degrading things about the people of the fellowship and their pastor. Many of the people of the church began to tune in to his radio broadcast to see what this man was saying about their church.

The more the man said, the worse his statements became. Many of the people of the church became upset with this man and held resentment against him. They even asked their pastor to go on the radio and publicly denounce his tormentor. The fundamentalist even challenged the pastor to a debate on doctrine.

This pastor is a devout man of God, who believes strongly in the unity of the body, and is an avid Bible scholar. Everyone in the congregation felt that if it came to a debate, their pastor could defeat the fundamentalist, hands down.

Several days went by with this particular radio preacher still attacking. He even attacked the way the pastor dressed and his overall appearance. The pastor refused to rise to the bait of a debate. He would not debate doctrine on the air waves for saints and sinners alike to hear two men of God arguing over the scriptures.

Instead, this pastor who was being attacked went on his regular radio broadcast and prayed for his counterpart, as well as the other pastors in that city, and for the unity of the body. He prayed for his brother and immediately *forgave* him for all the things he had said about him personally and the church as well.

The pastor's wife wrote the fundamentalist a letter asking for his forgiveness for whatever they had done to offend him. She invited him to their home for dinner.

The pastor stood before his congregation and told them they should, as a body, forgive the man for everything he had said about them. He led them collectively in a prayer of forgiveness.

This situation could have created a real problem in their fellowship had not their pastor acted in the manner he did. It would have been easy for him and other members of the body to hold a grudge against this man. Instead, as a united congregation, they prayed for this man and his church. It was a great lesson in forgiveness for the congregation as well as for others around the city.

Through forgiveness by the pastor and his congregation, the attacks stopped. God is still working in this man's heart and the entire city is learning more and more about forgiveness and its benefits.

Do you know that forgiveness can also bring revival to a church as well as a city? It can bring revival to you, because your well will be unstopped and God's Spirit will be able to again flow. It can also bring revival to others.

Revival once came to an entire church because of the forgiveness of a child.

An elder of the church was conducting the communion service one Sunday morning. He spoke on *purity in lives; making sure that your heart was right with God and with one another.*

There was an 11-year-old girl sitting on the pew listening intently as he spoke. He had very beady eyes that seemed to look right through you as he spoke. He said,

"Let a man examine his own heart and judge himself, lest he be judged by God." He warned about taking communion if you had anything in your heart against your brother or sister. "If you do, you are eating and drinking condemnation," he warned.

The young girl sitting quietly in the pew began to examine her heart. As she did, she discovered that she did have something in her heart against someone. Quickly she stood up and said, "I do!"

To the shock of everyone in the church, she began to cry and confessed that she had something in her heart against a woman in the church and wanted to ask her forgiveness.

The young girl went over to the woman in tears, threw her arms around her and began to ask her forgiveness.

THAT STARTED A REAL REVIVAL.

People began to stand and confess that they also had something in their heart against someone. Everyone was weeping, hugging, and rejoicing in the Lord.

Many of those people had something in their hearts that needed to be forgiven. But had it not been for this girl's courage, much of this would have gone unconfessed and unforgiven. They would have taken communion with all this unforgiveness still in their hearts. We wonder why God doesn't hear our prayers and we do not have revival. We could use a few more services like that in our churches today!

After that Sunday morning, with everyone weeping and forgiving one another, God's Spirit began to move. Not long after that there was a tremendous revival among the young people. All this came about through the forgiving heart of an 11-year-old girl.

FORGIVENESS RELEASES OTHERS so God can work with them. When we do not forgive people, we actually aid in binding them to their sins, restricting the working of the Holy Spirit in their salvation.

Twenty-two years ago, a promising young minister who was vice-president over a youth group began to think he should have been the president instead of the vice-president. Someone else was voted in over him for the second time and he began to build resentment and bitterness because he did not get the position he thought he should.

Stories were rumored about him that he had been threatening a bank president with physical harm. Could this be true? This man was a minister!

He is now in jail and on death row because he stabbed his wife and father-in-law.

This sad ending occurred because he was full of resentment and hatred. He gave place to the devil. He allowed Satan entry and with him he brought violence and murder.

We cannot afford to go around with a grudge. In Galations 5:15 the Bible says,

"But if ye bite and devour one another, take heed that ye be not consumed one of another."

THAT'S WHY WE HAVE TO FORGIVE.

Jesus said, *". . . Except your righteousness shall exceed the righteousness of the scribes and Pharisees, ye shall in no case enter into the kingdom of heaven." (Matt. 5:20)* The scribes and Pharisees paid their tithes, prayed and gave alms to those in need.

They were full of good works. So what was their problem? It was a self-righteous attitude. We need to be careful that we do not develop this kind of attitude. Peter asked how many times should I forgive, Lord? The Lord said 490 times. Many times you have to forgive the same people over and over again. It really wouldn't be forgiveness if you counted the number of times you forgave a person, would it? Forgiveness is genuinely saying, *"forget it."*

Matthew 5:44 says for us to *love* our enemies. Bless them that curse you. Pray for them that despitefully use you.

When you have feelings of resentment in your heart toward someone, *pray* for that person. Even if you don't feel it, do it because the Lord told you to. Within a few days you will be able to love that person and pray for them, truly meaning it.

When we are not right with each other, we are not right with God. In the First Epistle of John, chapter 4, verse 20 it says,

> *If a man say, I love God, and hateth his brother, he is a liar: for he that loveth not his brother whom he hath seen, how can he love God whom he hath not seen?*

I used to think to myself, "It's easy, because I have seen my brother and I don't love him." That isn't true. Our relationship with God is dependent on our relationship to our brother and sister. In the 21st verse it says:

> *And this commandment have we from him, That he who loveth God love his brother also.*

Loving your brother is a commandment! If you want all the rich blessings of God; if you want fellowship with your Heavenly Father; you must love your brother!

Chapter Eleven

FORGIVENESS THROUGH CONFESSION/ COMPLETE FORGIVENESS

In Matthew 12, Jesus talks about forgiveness and condemnation. If you can grasp onto the revelation of Christ
in you, alive *in* you, seated at the right hand of the
Father, your life can be changed. Verse 34 of Matthew 12
says:

> *O generation of vipers, how can ye, being
> evil, speak good things? for out of the
> abundance of the heart the mouth
> speaketh.*

Think about the last time somebody did you wrong.
What did you say the last time you mashed your finger in
the door? That is what fills your heart! We need to realize
what we are letting fill the abundance of our hearts.
Verses 35-37:

> *A good man out of the good treasure of
> the heart bringeth forth good things: and
> an evil man out of the evil treasure bring-
> eth forth evil things.*
>
> *But I say unto you, That every idle
> word that men shall speak, they shall give
> account thereof in the day of judgment.*
>
> *For by thy words thou shalt be justi-
> fied, and by thy words thou shalt be con-
> demned.*

What will happen if I say, "My wife is no good?"

What will happen if I say, "My kids are messed up kids?" The answer is obvious. I condemn them with my words!

I heard about a brother in the Lord who had a woman come to him and say: "My kid is fifteen years old. He has taken dope and is running with the wrong crowd. He has been in jail and now he is on probation." She went on for fifteen minutes about everything he was doing wrong.

"I know for sure he is going to end up in reform school. Would you pray for him every night?" she asked.

This brother said, "Lady, I won't even pray for him today. Until you are willing to straighten up your confession and start confessing what God is doing in the boy's life; until you are ready to start speaking *life* into him instead of condemnation, I cannot do anything to help you."

"I do not understand," she returned.

"You need to start confessing a little life into him, instead of jail and death and prison. You start confessing what God will do in his life, what he promised in his word, and things will start to change immediately."

PRAISE GOD!

Jesus said, *"He that believeth on me, as the scripture hath said, out of his belly shall flow rivers of living water." (John 7:38).* Have you ever thought about what those rivers of living water are? THE WORD OF GOD! It is the building up, the lifting up that is given unto us. That is what the man was trying to tell the mother of that boy.

"Sister, as long as you keep him bound with condemnation, God cannot set him free."

We are keeping a lot of people bound!

The thing we must do is start seeing people as Jesus sees them. It does not matter whether they are right or wrong. If you cannot love them as a brother, love them as an enemy. It is all the same. You are to love them.

Somewhere in that spectrum you can surely fit me, either as your brother or your enemy. And as you fit me, *love* me.

Jesus did not differentiate between the saved and the unsaved. He said if they heard his word and they did not obey it, he still did not judge them.

We sit up and say, I have made a rule. Anybody who does not hear my word, I judge. No! No! Judgment time is coming, but it is not now! Now is the time for speaking *life* into people!

My favorite scripture is in Colossians. Paul has written in Chapter 3, verses 11-17.

> *. . . but Christ is all, and in all.*
>
> *Put on therefore, as the elect of God, holy and beloved, bowels of mercies, kindness, humbleness of mind, meekness, long-suffering;*
>
> *Forbearing one another, and forgiving one another, if any man have a quarrel against any: even as Christ forgave you, so also do ye.*
>
> *And above all these things put on charity, which is the bond of perfectness.*
>
> *And let the peace of God rule in your hearts, to the which also ye are called in one body; and be ye thankful.*
>
> *Let the word of Christ dwell in you richly in all wisdom; teaching and ad- monishing one another in psalms and hymns and spiritual songs, singing with grace in your hearts to the Lord.*
>
> *And whatsoever ye do in word or deed, do all in the name of the Lord Jesus, giv- ing thanks to God and the Father by him.*

God called us to admonish our brother and to lift him up. TO LIFT HIM UP!

In Matthew 18:15-17 we read:

> *Moreover if thy brother shall trespass against thee, go and tell him his fault between thee and him alone: if he shall hear thee, thou hast gained thy brother.*
>
> *But if he will not hear thee, then take with thee one or two more, that in the mouth of two or three witnesses every word may be established.*
>
> *And if he shall neglect to hear them, tell it unto the church: but if he neglect to hear the church, let him be unto thee as an heathen man and a publican.*

I agree with that scripture. The problem is that we try to do the *third* step first. Jesus said for you to go to him yourself first. If we will start doing this, we will never have to take the second and third steps.

Jesus spoke about something very interesting in Matthew 18. He said whatever you loose on earth is loosed in heaven and whatever you bind on earth is bound in heaven. We can *loose* people right now, if we will only do it!

God so loved the world and he still loves the world. He says for you to do the same. Whosesoever sins you retain are retained; whosesoever sins you remit are remitted. Whatever you bind on earth is bound in heaven, whatever you loose on earth is loosed in heaven.

YOU CAN SET YOURSELF FREE, if you will be honest with yourself. I pray that the Holy Spirit will reveal to you anybody you need to forgive.

Don't sit around trying to guess who you need to forgive. The Holy Spirit knows your heart better than you do. If the Holy Spirit tells you to forgive your very best friend, do it. He knows what is in your heart.

Not long ago I prayed that the Holy Spirit would reveal to me anybody that I needed to forgive and I got a surprise. They were two of my very best friends in the ministry. If the Holy Spirit had not spoken to me after a time of prayer, I would have never believed it. I will tell you one thing though, when I forgave them, I got free and so did they!

The Lord brought it to my mind and I forgave them. Something released in me and the beautiful part is, I know something released in them too.

Listen to what the Holy Spirit says. FORGIVE YOURSELF! As you forgive yourself, peace will settle upon you. As you forgive yourself, nervousness will leave you. The Bible tells us to be anxious about nothing and this can come about through FORGIVENESS OF OURSELVES.

God is calling the body to a forgiving heart, one that is full of forgiveness. That is when the *power* is going to come.

If you will not forgive, your power supply is going to get cut off. We are starting to see it happen in churches.

If you will not forgive, your prosperity is going to get cut off.

If you will not forgive, your healing will not manifest itself.

A man came to me recently with tears rolling down his cheeks, "Gene, what are we going to do about our church?"

I asked him to explain.

They had had a Spirit-filled group in their church ministering and *everybody* loved it. One of the spectators, during the time of praise, prayed ever so quietly in tongues. One of the church people heard him. They judged the group ministering and threw them out of the church and will not let them minister there again.

This man said to me, "What can we do? Our church now is only about a third the size it was."

I said, "Start forgiving, so the Lord can come back in."

We are coming to a time when we are going to get hot or cold. You may as well get ready for it.

It does not make any difference who is right and who is wrong. That is unimportant. The only thing involved is *you* as a forgiver!

Sinner or Christian is not even involved. FORGIVE!

When we see people sinning, we need to be right there, forgiving them, so God can work in their lives.

When God revealed that to me, I ran into my house, grabbed my kids and my wife and said, "I forgive you for everything you have ever done." Hallelujah! Praise God!

I WANTED THEM TO BE FREE!

Not only did I want them to be free, but I want you to be free too. God will do things in your heart for you, if you will allow him to! Get yourself loosed and loose others in the process. Remember, as *you* forgive it shall be forgiven you!

Get that hardness out of your heart. As you read along in the next paragraph of this book, make it a prayer of yours to the Lord Jesus Christ:

"Father, in the name of Jesus, I pray that your Holy Spirit minister right now in my life. Look upon my heart for any malice, any slander, or anything against my brother or my sister or anyone else, whether they are in the family of God or not. Lord, I ask that any unforgiveness against anyone be brought to my mind right now by the power of your Holy Spirit. I start forgiving now, each and every one you have brought to mind. (If it be wives, husbands, kids, bosses, ex-wives, ex-husbands, Christian brother or sister that you have had an argument with, or whatever, just forgive.) I come against every spirit of unforgiveness in the name of Jesus, and bind it right now. I pray that your forgiveness will flow through me. Lord, I praise you for what you are doing in my heart right now."

If you have prayed this prayer sincerely, unashamedly, and will follow the leading of the Holy Spirit, your life has already been changed. I challenge you, if you are having a battle in your Christian life, be aware of what the Holy Spirit is saying to you. If he is not saying anything to you, then look at yourself.

Have I forgiven myself? Can I look upon the world as Jesus did and say, "Father, forgive them?" Can I look at that crowd that did me so wrong, as Stephen did, and say, *"Don't charge them with this sin." Am I doing that?*

Ask yourself these questions. BE HONEST WITH YOURSELF!

If you have been honest then *forgiveness* is now the state of your heart. FAMILIES CAN NOW BE RESTORED! Now you are free and many others are free too!

It takes a great revelation of Jesus Christ for us to have a forgiving heart. It takes a great revelation of Jesus Christ to be able to love everyone that we see. I pray that through this book YOU HAVE TRULY FORGIVEN!

And now that you have forgiven, what next? The next time your wife or husband speaks short to you will you then again harbor unforgiveness? When your teenager berates you, will you respond in kind? When the boss jumps on you undeservedly, what will your response be?

In the 4th chapter of Mark, Jesus is teaching on the parable of the Sower of Seed. Beginning with the 4th verse, He said:

> *"And it came to pass, as he sowed, some fell by the way side, and the fowls of the air came and devoured it up.*
>
> *And some fell on stony ground, where it had not much earth; and immediately it sprang up, because it had no depth of earth:*
>
> *But when the sun was up, it was scorched; and because it had no root, it withered away.*

> *And some fell among thorns, and the*
> *thorns grew up, and choked it, and it*
> *yielded no fruit.*
>
> *And other fell on good ground, and did*
> *yield fruit that sprang up and increased;*
> *and brought forth, some thirty, and some*
> *sixty, and some an hundred."*

And he said unto them, "He that hath ears to hear, let him hear." (Are your spiritual ears tuned in to hear the truths?)

When Jesus had finished teaching and was alone with the disciples they asked him the meaning of the parable. He patiently answered them, starting with verse 14:

"The sower soeth the word."

(I want you to think on this! This book has sown the word on forgiveness. If you have received the word you have now forgiven. Now will you bring forth fruit?)

Verse 15 continues:

> *And these are they by the way side, where*
> *the word is sown; but when they have*
> *heard, Satan cometh immediately, and*
> *taketh away the word that was sown in*
> *their hearts.*

(The word is now in your heart, do not allow Satan to steal it − hold tightly to the truth you have gained.)

> *And these are they likewise which are*
> *sown on stony ground; who, when they*
> *have heard the word, immediately receive*
> *it with gladness;*
>
> *And have no root in themselves, and so*
> *endure but for a time; afterward, when*
> *affliction or persecution ariseth for the*
> *word's sake, immediately they are of-*
> *fended."*

(If somebody berates you, will you be offended, and having endured but for a time, wither away?)

Verse 18 goes on:

> *And these are they which are sown among*
> *thorns; such as hear the word,*

> *And the cares of this world, and the deceitfulness of riches, and the lusts of other things entering in, choke the word, and it becometh unfruitful."*

(The cares of the world, or worries, along with lusts for other things of the world, choke the word! Be aware of this and do not allow it to happen to you.)

The 20th verse sums it all up as follows:

> *And these are they which are sown on good ground; such as hear the word, and receive it, and bring forth fruit, some thirty-fold, some sixty, and some an hundred.*

What will your return in fruit be? Will it be 30 percent, 60 percent, or 100 percent? That depends entirely on you. Hold fast to your confession and do not waver and resist the devil and he will flee from you.

When affliction or persecution arises for the word's sake, how will you take that? When you forgive someone and it seems to do no good at all what will you do? Will you continue to believe God's word or will you immediately be offended and start to question God? Remember, if you hold fast you will reap 100 percent.

When the worries of the world, the state of the nation, the search for riches (the deceitful promise of security) and the search or desire for other things, enters in, will you allow them to throttle the word of God?

YOU HAVE HEARD THE WORD, NOW ASSIMILATE IT, HOLDING FAST TO YOUR CONFESSION. RESISTING SATAN. RESISTING ALL PERSECUTION, RESISTING ALL WORRY, AND REAP 100 percent!